Bu

THE BEST
BIKE RIDES
IN
NEW ENGLAND

THE BEST BIKE RIDES IN NEW ENGLAND

by
Paul D. Thomas

AN EAST WOODS BOOK

The
Globe
Pequot
Press

Chester, Connecticut

Library of Congress Cataloging-in-Publication Data

Thomas, Paul D. (Paul Dudley)
    The best bike rides in New England : from Nantucket Sound to Lake Champlain, from the Berkshires to Mount Desert, more than 2,000 miles of adventure for the active cyclist / by Paul D. Thomas. — 1st ed.
        p. cm.
    "An East Woods book."
    ISBN 0-87106-471-5
    1. Bicycle touring—New England—Guide-books. 2. New England—Description and travel—1981—Guide-books. I. Title.
GV1045.5.N36T46 1990
796.6'4'0974—dc20
                                                              89-49745
                                                              CIP

Manufactured in the United States of America
First Edition/First Printing

for Sarah

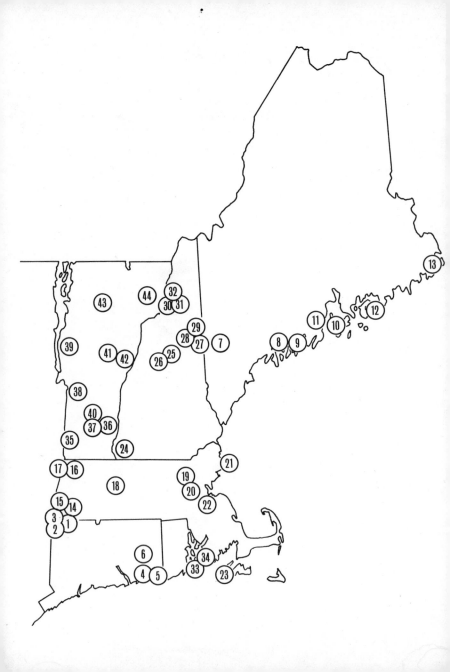

Contents

Introduction

Bike Rides

Appendix: Bicycle Touring and Racing Clubs in New England

Introduction

The Best Bike Rides in New England

Massachusetts isn't only the cradle of liberty—it's the birthplace of bicycling in America. The Boston Bicycle Club, founded in 1878 by fourteen high-wheeled cyclists, was the country's very first bike club. Its first ride went from Boston to Brookline.

New England can boast of other cycling firsts as well. According to *The Wheel,* a popular cycling journal of the day, "The first bicycle rider in this country was Alfred Chandler, now a eminent Boston lawyer." The first "remarkable ride" was W. R. Pitman's tour from Boston to Haverhill, a distance exceeding 42 miles, which he covered in five hours and forty minutes. That must have been a great training ride, for Pitman went on to win "the first amateur race," run at Lynn, Massachusetts, on July 4, 1878.

If only these two gentlemen were with us today. They could trade in their hundred-pound high-wheelers for high-performance machines, exchange their wool knickers for Lycra cycling shorts, and enjoy weekly races and "remarkable rides" the whole year round. For company on the road, they could join any of several dozen New England–area racing and touring clubs. To revisit some of their familiar haunts, they might sign up for a weekend-long, inn-to-inn cycling expedition, during which they could rest every night in lodgings that were historical even a hundred years ago.

Reflecting the new vitality and sophistication of cycling in its second century, *The Best Bike Rides in New England* is the first all-new guide to cycling the entire six-state region published in fifteen years. Today's cyclists include weekend tourists and competitive racers alike, women and men who want to know where the best rides are—where the roads offer beautiful and varied scenery, challenges they can rise to, a perfect day of solitude or camaraderie.

Regional cycling clubs, inn-to-inn tour leaders, racing teams, coaches, and a host of cycling fans have contributed their favorites to this collection of forty-five tours. Ranging in length from 20 to more than 100 miles, the best bike rides in New England have proven appeal to active weekend riders and competitive racers alike.

Here's a short sample:

● "The Allis Loop" is the all-time favorite training ride of John Allis, three-time Olympic cyclist and Boston area racing coach.

● "Acadia Carriage Path Cruise," tackled every April by Maine's Penobscot Bay Wheelmen, has special appeal for New England's growing number of mountain bike enthusiasts.

● "Northeast Kingdom Challenge" includes the unanimous favorite ride of tour leaders at the Vermont Country Cyclers company, one of New England's famous tour operators. The folks from Vermont Bicycle Touring and Maine Coast Cyclers have also chipped in a selection of their most popular rides.

● "Bash Bish Falls Tri-State Challenge" is one of a quartet of Berkshire tours that explore the author's favorite corner of New England.

● Before pedaling down the road, review the following tips. They will help make every ride a great ride.

Tips toward a Safer and More Exhilarating Ride

Riding a bicycle, a combination of sport, transportation, and exploration, can be a rewarding and exhilarating experience. Mental, physical, and material preparation, though, are critical to safety and enjoyment. Experts have written volumes about touring and racing technique, training strategy, bicycle maintenance, and sports nutrition. Cycling magazines publish regular features on these topics and countless others. The most important lessons, however, can be summarized in the following tips. Cyclists just beginning to ride distances longer than 20 miles should read these carefully. Even the most experienced rider can benefit from a quick review.

Pace yourself to last the distance. On long tours, start out slowly. You will have plenty of time to test your speed once you have stretched out, warmed up, and settled into the ride.

• If you are tackling a longer ride for the first time, don't hesitate to stop and enjoy some of the scenery along the way. Dismount, stretch, and walk around every 10 or 20 miles. You'll find that you can ride comfortably for hours if you take these short breaks.

• Drink plenty of water as you ride. Take frequent small sips, drinking much more often than you feel you need to. It's easy to become dehydrated on a long ride, because the breeze you create helps evaporate perspiration. Never wait for signs of thirst before taking a pull from your water bottle.

Tune up your cycling technique. Here are some pointers to help you go farther faster with less energy.

• Use the full range of your pedal stroke. Toe clips and cycling shoes will help you apply even pressure throughout the pedal's revolution. Focus on pulling up with one pedal as you push down on the other. This will result in a smoother and much faster ride.

• Maintain higher RPMs. You should pedal at a cadence of about ninety revolutions per minute. This means selecting a relatively easy gear and spinning your cranks. This may seem awkward at first, but you will soon get used to it and appreciate why racers often train in this manner. The inexperienced rider tends to push too hard a gear too early in a ride, placing stress on the knees and the lower back. Maintaining a high pedal revolution provides a better aerobic workout for your heart and lungs.

• On long climbs, alternate between sitting and spinning in a low gear and standing on the pedals to push a higher gear. If you feel like walking up a particularly tough climb, try stopping for a minute-long stretch and then remounting your bike to try again. The secret to making it up any climb is to always use a lower gear than you need. Start out easy and increase your pace only as you near the top.

• Relax your elbows and shoulders, and vary your hand position. Grip your handlebars on top, around the brake hoods, in the drops, and at every point in between. Keeping your arms loose and alternating your hand position often helps to ward off muscle fatigue on longer rides.

• Brake in short bursts to avoid locking up your wheels. Use both front and rear brakes. Because your front brake catches your forward momentum, it provides more braking power than your rear brake.

Share the road with others, as you would have them share it with you.

• Obey traffic laws, not only for your own safety but also to earn the respect of drivers. Use brief stops at traffic lights to drink water, stretch, or wait for your riding partners to catch up.

• Ride to be predictable. Ride single file on the right side of the road. Never swerve suddenly into the road. Use hand signals. This is just common sense. Cars signal turns and stops, and cyclists should too.

• Turning left is the most dangerous maneuver in bicycling. Always look behind you before turning left, taking care that you don't drift into the road as you do so. Never turn left suddenly from the far right side of the road. When approaching a left turn, move to the left turn lane or the center of the road after checking for traffic behind you. On busy roads, pull off to the right, onto the road's shoulder, and wait until traffic is clear in both directions before crossing. A rearview mirror attached to your left handlebar plug or your helmet will help you keep an eye on traffic.

Wear a helmet. It could save your life.

• Contemporary cycling helmets are feather-light, well ventilated, extremely comfortable, and appealing. There is no excuse for not wearing one. A good helmet can cost more than $50, but it is also your single most important investment in the sport. Don't skimp on safety.

Equip yourself properly. Ride prepared for every contingency.

• It is not necessary to own an expensive bicycle to enjoy riding. It is important, though, that whatever bike you ride be well maintained and safe. Make certain that your brakes and derailleurs are adjusted properly. Spray and wipe your chain regularly with a light-grade lubricant. Check your tires for embedded bits of glass and stone before every ride.

• Carry a pump and a spare tire or tube on every ride. Know how to fix a flat tire. Riding through glass can either cause a minor annoyance or ruin your ride, depending on how prepared you are.

• Carry some personal identification, a few extra dollars, and change for a telephone call. Many experienced riders keep these items in a waterproof sandwich bag to carry on every ride. If you are cycling alone from a vacation home, a friend's house, or a hotel or inn, always jot down the address, phone number, and your name on a piece of paper to slip in your jersey pocket before you set out.

• Considering the unpredictability of New England weather, it's a wise idea to carry a lightweight, packable rain jacket on spring and fall rides. This item will fit easily into a small pack that attaches beneath your bicycle seat.

Adjust your bike so it fits. Don't let it misadjust you.

• Saddle height and tilt are the most critical factors for a comfortable riding position. When the balls of your feet are on the pedals, your knees should be just slightly bent at the bottom of each stroke. Your seat is too high if your hips rock as you pedal. To determine your saddle's proper tilt, balance a yardstick lengthwise along its nose and back. The stick should be level, parallel to your bike's top tube. Many riders make the mistake of tilting their seats slightly forward, thrusting too much weight and stress onto their shoulders, arms, and hands.

• Your reach to the handlebars and your handlebar height are also important. When you are in the normal riding position with your hands on your brake hoods, your front wheel's hub should be hidden behind or just visible in front of your handlebars' cross section. Overextending your back and arms to reach your bars will cause discomfort and stiffness. The top of your bars should be level with or about 1 inch below the top of your seat.

• An increasing number of bike shops now offer precision fitting services to adjust your bicycle to your body proportions. If you are having difficulty finding a comfortable riding position, consult a quality bike shop in your area.

Dress for the sport. Bicycle clothing is more than a current fashion craze. Proper shorts, jerseys, shoes, and gloves, besides looking good, provide a more comfortable ride. None of these items are absolutely necessary; but, on a longer ride especially, you'll be glad you are wearing them.

• Skintight shorts, most commonly black but now sold in a rainbow of colors, prevent chafing and provide a more aerodynamic profile. They also provide padding at those vital contact points.

• Bright jerseys make you visible on the road, and the pockets in back are convenient for carrying your wallet, some food, and a map (or this book).

• Cycling shoes are available in racing or touring models. Both feature stiff soles that provide more comfort and transfer more of your leg power to the pedals. Proper cycling shoes also feature special grooves or cleats that securely engage the pedals for steady leg power all around the stroke.

• Padded gloves absorb road shock and protect against abrasions should you stop a fall with the palm of your hand.

• Eyewear for cycling shields against sun, wind, bugs, and dirt. Wear sunglasses, or choose specially designed cycling glasses that have interchangeable light and dark lenses.

• Always wear more rather than less. In raw weather the wind you create while riding will accentuate the cold. Riding in cold conditions can be fun, but only if you dress appropriately. Wear a cap beneath your helmet. Cotton gardening gloves that fit over regular cycling gloves are an inexpensive substitute for winter cycling gloves. Wear a second jersey, or a sweatshirt, sweater, or jacket. Wool or polypropylene cycling tights will keep your legs warm. A quality bike shop is the best source for winter clothing designed specifically for the sport.

Practice group riding etiquette. The company of other riders can make any tour more enjoyable. Riding in a group, though, requires extra attention and a certain amount of courtesy.

• Whether you are an experienced cyclist comfortable with drafting in the slipstream of others or a recreational cyclist out with a large group for the first time, obey these five rules: Always ride in a straight line, avoiding any sudden swerves to either side. Never stop suddenly; if you must stop, pull all the way off the road to the right. Riding in a tight group, point out obstacles, shouting "glass," "rocks," and so forth. Warn other cyclists of an approaching car by shouting "car back" or "car up." Never ride through a traffic light, and never make a left turn in traffic unless the whole group can make it at once.

• Arrive prepared for the ride. Don't make others wait while you take care of adjustments that should have been made earlier. Carry a pump, spare tire, cash, food, and water. Don't count on borrowing any of these from another rider.

Eat well on and off the bike.

• Eat small snacks on rides longer than two hours. You need to replace the blood sugar depleted through constant exertion. Bananas, oranges, raisins, and candy bars are favorite on-the-bike snacks of experienced cyclists. Many riders also swear by glucose- or fructose-based drinks.

• Don't combine cycling and dieting. Dieting will sap you of needed strength. And anyway, if you ride regularly, dieting will be unnecessary.

• Minimize your alcohol intake for at least two days before a big ride. Alcohol disturbs your body's chemistry and makes you more susceptible to becoming dehydrated while you ride.

Know your limits. Don't bite off more than you can chew.

• A long ride requires preparation and training. Never ride a tour more than 20 miles longer than one you have ridden comfortably before. All of the rides in this book are divided into Rambles (easy), Cruises (intermediate), Challenges (difficult), and Classics (expert). If you are just beginning to ride longer distances, work your way up through these categories. Always begin your season with many short rides ridden in an easy gear.

Get (and stay) fit. The pleasure you get out of cycling will increase in direct proportion to your level of fitness.

- Racers ride over 300 miles per week in daily training sessions. Don't worry about trying to match that pace, but do think about getting some form of exercise every day. Jog, swim, play tennis, attend aerobics classes—do anything to get your heart and lungs working hard for at least a half hour every day. And keep up your regimen throughout the winter to get a head start on the next cycling season.

- The best way to train for cycling, of course, is to ride regularly. Don't limit cycling to weekends. Commute by bike, or throw the bike in your car for a short lunchtime ride. Even a half-hour spin a few times during the week will improve your stamina and strengthen your legs.

- If you are a competitive cyclist, be careful not to overtrain. Riding hard every day can easily result in physical and mental fatigue. Take one day off every week, perhaps using the opportunity to play softball, volleyball, or any other sport with your noncycling friends.

Get your mind right, too. Mental fitness is as important as physical ability.

- One cycling magazine conducted a poll of its readers that showed attitude to be as important as fitness to the enjoyment of bike riding. Before you set off, prepare yourself mentally for the challenge ahead. Visualize the ride. If you have never ridden the course before, study the map and directions so that you will know where the difficult stretches are and can pace yourself accordingly. *Don't be goaded by others into riding a tour that you feel unprepared for.*

- Search out new rides. Every rider has his or her favorite local loop, but exploring new routes can make cycling fresher and more adventurous. Start with some of the rides in this book. Plan a cycling weekend in the Berkshires or the White Mountains, by the Atlantic or along Lake Champlain. The exhilaration you feel in cycling through newly discovered countryside will carry over into your regular neighborhood rides.

Join a club.

• Touring clubs, most of which are affiliated with the League of American Wheelmen, organize regular weekend and occasional weekday evening rides throughout the year. These are often listed in local newspapers. Touring clubs also publish newsletters, organize rallies, offer equipment discounts, and host dinners throughout the year.

• If you are interested in cycling competitively, join a racing club. There is no substitute for the formal and informal coaching, training rides, races, and cycling clinics that are a part of most club programs. Larger clubs offer programs for all levels of cyclists.

• This book's appendix presents a state-by-state listing of New England's established touring and racing clubs. Contact the League of American Wheelmen or the United States Cycling Federation for additional information about clubs in your area.

How to Use This Book

The Best Bike Rides in New England places each ride in one of four categories according to the ride's degree of difficulty—easy, intermediate, difficult, or expert. Each ride's name indicates its rating.

Rambles are this collection's easiest rides, perfect for the beginning cyclist or for the experienced rider looking for a relaxed, scenic outing. All Rambles are less than 35 miles long and cover flat or rolling terrain.

Cruises are intermediate rides for those ready to test their legs over moderate distances and eager to tackle a hill or two. Cruises generally measure between 25 and 50 miles and cross rolling or hilly terrain.

Challenges require adequate training and preparation beforehand. These 40- to 70-mile routes commonly feature long climbs that, however scenic, may prove too difficult for the inexperienced cyclist. But the active rider should view these tours, which explore some of New England's most picturesque regions, as welcome challenges.

Classics are the black diamond slopes of bicycling. Most Classics earn this rating, though, less for the steepness of their descents than for the difficulty of their climbs or for their sheer length. Classic rides are generally over 60 miles long and cross hilly or mountainous terrain. Some shorter rides, such as the Mount Greylock Classic, qualify for this experts-only rating as well.

Most rides offer shorter and longer options; these options are noted in their directions. Some Challenges, for example, feature shorter loops that would qualify as Cruises or even Rambles. In selecting a ride, look not only at its rating but also at the different lengths of its various options.

Keep in mind that these ratings represent guidelines rather than rules. What may be a fun, moderately challenging ride for one rider can prove an unpleasant endurance test for another. Remember: Know your limits and be careful not to set out for a tour that is twice as long or hilly as any you have ever completed. Read each ride's description and directions before rolling down the road. All major climbs are noted so that you may pace yourself appropriately.

For each ride in this book, directions include the cumulative mileage at each turn. One small and relatively inexpensive piece of equipment will help you keep track of your mileage and will make these directions easier to follow. This is a cyclometer, essentially a digital wristwatch for your bike's handlebars. Besides telling time, a cyclometer displays your speed and the elapsed distance for a ride. More sophisticated and expensive models can also display your cadence, or the rate of revolution for your pedals, and your heart rate.

Your bike shop is likely to carry a half dozen different cyclometer brands. The simplest models, which display trip distance, speed, and time, are generally the least expensive and most reliable. The Avocet, favored by most racers, is one of these. It is particularly compact, about the size of an Oreo cookie, and costs approximately $35.

Acknowledgments

This book could never have been written without the generous contributions, comments, and moral support of individuals, clubs, and cycling organizations throughout New England. I would like to thank in particular Dennis and Ellen Curran of Maine Coast Cyclers; Bob Maynard of Vermont Country Cyclers; Bill Perry and Steve Bushey of Vermont Bicycle Touring; Linda Harvey and Adolphe Bernotas of the Granite State Wheelmen; all the folks with my local club, the Charles River Wheelmen; Wally Bugbee and Ken Bell, ride leaders for the Penobscot Wheelmen; John Fletcher of the Pequot Cyclists; Al Lester of the American Youth Hostels, Greater Boston Council; Mike Farney of the Lincoln Guide Service shop; coach and teacher Leif Thorne-Thomsen; and John Allis, who actually pushed me the final 5 miles back to his Belmont Wheel Works shop after my back and legs had given out for the day.

My thanks also to the countless shopkeepers, innkeepers, motorists, and passersby whom I met while scouting out these routes. Whether offering directions, advising me of road conditions ahead, or providing a hot cup of coffee on a cold day, you all contributed immeasurably to this effort.

Disclaimer

The Globe Pequot Press assumes no liability for accidents happening to, or injuries sustained by, readers who engage in the activities described in this book.

Connecticut

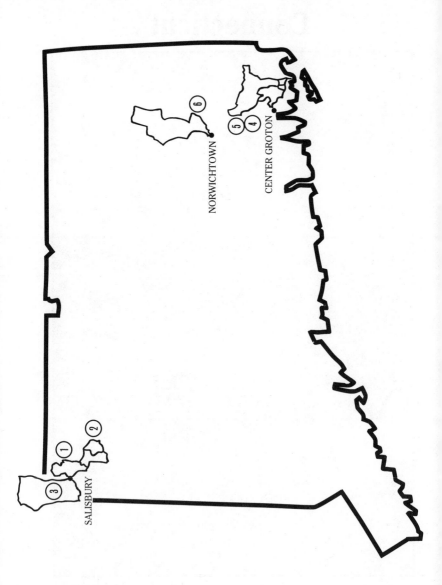

Connecticut

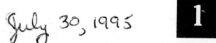

1

Twin Lakes Ramble

Salisbury—Lime Rock—Falls Village
Salisbury

The rolling roads of the Housatonic Valley in Connecticut's far northwest corner provide the ideal setting for a long weekend of cycling. The Twin Lakes Ramble, Music Mountain Cruise, and Bash Bish Falls Tri-State Challenge all start and end in the town of Salisbury, only two hours north but a world away from New York City. So pack your bags and bikes for a weekend in the southern Berkshires. Book yourself into one of the many local inns or bed and breakfast accommodations. Then follow these three rides through the flatlands and hills surrounding Connecticut's "Hoosie River."

Starting from Salisbury, where the town fountain provides springwater for your fuel, the Twin Lakes Ramble leads first to the town of Lime Rock, home of actor Paul Newman's favorite auto racing track. Pause at the Lime Rock Park gates to watch some of the action.

Although you are more likely to hear the high-pitched whine of high-performance engines, the track has in the past hosted bicycle races as well. Veterans of the Lime Rock cycling series will regale you with tales of "The Wall" on the backstretch and will try to find words for the supercharged feeling of sprinting for the checkered flag on the final pass down the long, skid-marked straightaway.

From Lime Rock, this course crosses over the Housatonic

River itself. It passes alongside the river for just over a mile, at the end of which there is a grassy bank and picnic area overlooking kayak gates strung across the water. This is the best spot along the route to pause; you can eat any snacks you may have packed while watching the kayakers paddle their nimble craft through the river's rapids.

Next destination: the Twin Lakes that lend this ride their name. Lakes Washining and Washinee lie only a quarter mile apart, the bulge of one fitting into the curve of the other. Twin Lakes Road and then Taconic Road trace a rolling route around this pair, ending in Route 44, just a mile-long coast north of the public fountain in Salisbury center.

If you time your visit to coincide with the annual Salisbury Antiques Fair, you can look forward to spending the rest of the day browsing through the tents raised all along either side of Main Street.

The Basics

Start: Salisbury, the most northwesterly town in Connecticut. From New York, follow Rte. 22 to Millerton, then turn east on Rte. 44 into Connecticut and through Lakeville to Salisbury. From Connecticut or Massachusetts, follow Rte. 7 to Canaan, then turn west onto Rte. 44 into Salisbury. Combined routes 44 and 41 become Main St. Park on either side or behind the new Town Hall at the town's southern end.
Length: 20.2 miles.
Terrain: Mildly rolling roads; no major climbs.
Food: Salisbury is the biggest town on this ride. You may want to pack a snack to eat on the grassy banks of the Housatonic, by the kayak gates spanning the river at 7.2 miles, or at the Twin Lakes dock at 14.1 miles.

Miles and Directions

- 0.0 Start at Salisbury Town Hall, in town center on west side of combined routes 44 and 41, here named Main St. Fill water

Twin Lakes Road

Twin Lakes Road

Twin Lakes

41

Taconic Road

Weatogue Road

44

Belden Street

126

N

41/44

SALISBURY

Start/finish at
public fountain
in Salisbury

Housatonic River

41/44

Lime Rock Road

Brewster Street

FALLS VILLAGE

7

Lake
Wonomscopomuc

Dugway Road

LIME
ROCK

112

Lime Rock
Race Track

bottles at spring-fed fountain. Ride south on Main St. toward Lakeville.

- 0.1 Turn left off Main Street, just beyond town center, onto Lime Rock Rd.
- 2.2 Continuing on Lime Rock Rd., pass turnoff to Lakeville on right.
- 3.4 Stay right with Lime Rock Rd., riding alongside Salmon Creek on the right.
- 4.2 Left onto Rte. 112, Town Hill Rd., at T after quick downhill.
- 4.4 Enter Lime Rock, continuing straight on Rte. 112 as White Hollow Rd. bears off to right.
- 5.2 Left onto Dugway Rd., toward Amesville, directly opposite entrance to Lime Rock Park motor speedway.
- 7.4 Right, toward Rte. 7, onto the blue iron trestle bridge crossing the Housatonic. Stay right on Water St. coming off the bridge.
- 7.7 Prepare for three successive left turns: Stay left with Water St. as it passes beneath stone railway bridge; turn left immediately thereafter onto Point of Rocks Rd.; then turn left onto Rte. 126N, here named Brewster St.
- 9.3 Bear left with Rte. 126 as it crosses railroad tracks. Sand Rd. bears off to right.
- 11.3 Left on Rte. 44, passing over short stone bridge over Housatonic.
- 11.6 Right onto Weatogue Rd., the first turn after crossing the river.
- 12.1 Left onto Twin Lakes Rd.
- 14.1 Stay left on Twin Lakes Rd. after passing public boat launch area on left.
- 14.6 Stay left again where Cooper Hill Rd. joins from the right.
- 15.9 Bear left at fork, staying on Twin Lakes Rd. Then turn left, toward Salisbury and Lakeville, at the stop sign that immediately follows.
- 16.3 Continue straight at intersection. Twin Lakes Rd. becomes Taconic Rd.

- 18.8 Right onto Rte. 44 at end of Taconic Rd. Ride on the shoulder here, as the traffic is fast.
- 20.0 Enter Salisbury, passing the White Hart Inn on the right as Rte. 44 merges into Rte. 41 south.
- 20.2 Arrive back at Salisbury Town Hall.

2

Music Mountain Cruise

Salisbury—Lime Rock—Falls Village
Cornwall—West Cornwall
Lime Rock—Salisbury

The Music Mountain Cruise rolls south from Salisbury to West Cornwall. Here, when autumn sets the foliage ablaze, a covered bridge across the Housatonic River attracts just about as many visitors as this small village wedged between the hills can handle. Cars line up along Route 7, and weekending New Yorkers crowd the few stores. Hikers and campers on their way into the surrounding woods pass through the bridge. Fishermen cast for trout lurking in the shadows of its span, and kayakers float by. The Music Mountain Cruise descends into this throng, providing an exhilarating interlude midway through an otherwise quiet ride.

This is the second of three rides starting and ending in the southern Berkshires town of Salisbury. This ride follows the same path as the shorter Twin Lakes Ramble as far as Falls Village. From there, however, it diverges to explore the hills and river valley farther south.

Just outside Falls Village the Music Mountain Cruise divides, offering two options for arriving in West Cornwall. The shorter ride turns right on a back road to climb Music Mountain, a green knob rising abruptly from the river. The route passes through a magnificent century-old row of sugar maples leading to a hilltop dairy farm and then plunges down the other side. This first option makes up for the miles saved with its moderately steep 3-mile climb. The longer option skirts Music Mountain and requires only a short climb after 10 gradually rolling miles.

The two routes rejoin on the descent into West Cornwall, then follow the Housatonic River back through Lime Rock to West Cornwall.

The Basics

Start: Salisbury, the most northwesterly town in Connecticut. From New York, follow Rte. 22 to Millerton, then turn east on Rte. 44 into Connecticut and through Lakeville to Salisbury. From Connecticut or Massachusetts, follow Rte. 7 to Canaan, then turn west onto Rte. 44 into Salisbury. Combined routes 44 and 41 become Main St. Park on either side or behind the new Town Hall at the town's southern end.
Length: 29.9 or 33.9 miles.
Terrain: Rolling roads. The shorter option crosses Music Mountain, a challenging 3-mile climb in two big steps. The longer option skirts this obstacle and features only one short climb.
Food: The covered bridge at West Cornwall is an ideal spot to stop for a rest and a bite to eat. Either pack your snack or visit one of the village's small stores to see what they offer. There are picnic tables on the grassy riverbank to the right just before the bridge.

Miles and Directions

- 0.0 Start at Salisbury Town Hall, in town center on west side of combined routes 41 and 44, here named Main Street. Ride south on Main St. toward Lakeville.
- 0.1 Turn left off Main St., just beyond town center, onto Lime Rock Rd.
- 2.2 Continuing on Lime Rock Rd., pass turnoff to Lakeville on right.

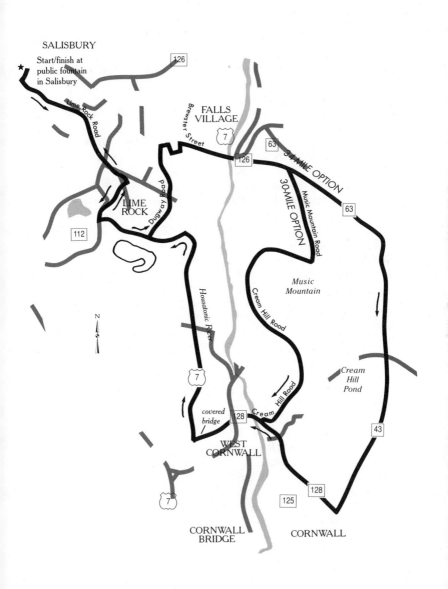

SALISBURY

Start/finish at
public fountain
in Salisbury

126

Lime Rock Road

FALLS
VILLAGE

Brewster Street

7

63

34-MILE OPTION

126

LIME
ROCK

Dugway Road

30-MILE OPTION

Music Mountain Road

63

112

Music
Mountain

Cream Hill Road

Cream
Hill
Pond

N

Housatonic River

7

Cream Hill Road

43

covered
bridge

128

Cream

WEST
CORNWALL

7

128

125

CORNWALL
BRIDGE

CORNWALL

- 3.4 Stay right with Lime Rock Rd., riding alongside Salmon Creek on the right.
- 4.2 Left on Rte. 112, Town Hill Rd., at T after a quick downhill.
- 4.4 Enter Lime Rock, continuing straight on Rte. 112 as White Hollow Rd. bears off to right.
- 5.2 Left onto Dugway Rd., toward Amesville, directly opposite entrance to Lime Rock Park motor speedway.
- 7.4 Turn right, toward Rte. 7, onto the blue iron trestle bridge crossing the Housatonic. Stay right on Water St. coming off the bridge.
- 7.7 Prepare for two left turns: Stay left with Water St. as it passes beneath stone railway bridge; turn left immediately thereafter onto Point of Rocks Rd.; then turn right onto Rte. 126, here named Brewster St. (This is where the Twin Lakes Ramble turns left.)
- 8.2 Cross Rte. 7, continuing straight.
- 9.7 Merge right onto Rte. 63.

From here, the two options to this ride diverge. The shorter ride makes up for the miles saved with a moderately steep climb for the next 3 miles. The longer option skirts the hills to your right and requires only a short climb 10 miles from here. The two routes rejoin on the descent into West Cornwall.

Option One
- 9.8 Turn right onto Music Mountain Rd. almost immediately after merging into Rte. 63.
- 13.8 Turn sharp left, uphill, onto Cream Hill Rd. Be careful not to follow Music Mountain Rd. downhill to the right.
- 16.2 Sharp right at bottom of long, steep descent, staying on Cream Hill Rd. Approach turn with caution. Continue straight through intersection in 1 mile.
- 17.5 Merge right onto Rte. 128, a well-paved road that swoops downhill to the Housatonic. (Option Two joins here from the left.)
- 19.0 Slow down for the blind curve into West Cornwall at

bottom of descent. Weekends see a lot of sightseers on the street here.

- 19.1 Cross covered bridge over the Housatonic and turn right onto Rte. 7N toward Lime Rock and Canaan. Rte. 7 rolls along the western side of the Housatonic for the next 5 miles.
- 23.9 Turn left at the short cutoff to Rte. 112 toward Lime Rock. Watch out for traffic from both directions here.
- 24.7 Pass the Lime Rock Park raceway on the left and begin to retrace route to Salisbury.
- 25.7 Right onto Lime Rock Rd. Follow winding route for next 4 miles.
- 29.8 Right onto combined routes 41 and 44 into Salisbury.
- 29.9 Return to Salisbury public fountain.

Option Two

- 9.7 Continue straight on Rte. 63 toward Cornwall Hollow and Goshen after merge.
- 13.5 Bear right onto Rte. 43, Great Hollow Rd., toward Cornwall Hollow and Cornwall.
- 15.0 Continue straight through village of Cornwall Hollow.
- 18.8 Turn right on Rte. 128 toward West Cornwall.
- 20.1 Stay right with Rte. 128 as Rte. 125 joins from the left.
- 21.5 Continue straight as the Option One route, Cream Hill Rd., merges into Rte. 128 from the right.
- 23.0 Slow down for the blind curve into West Cornwall at bottom of descent. From here, turn right onto Rte. 7, following the directions under Option One, starting at 19.1 miles, back to Salisbury. Just add 4 miles to the mileage at each direction. That's the extra distance you've picked up by circling rather than climbing Music Mountain.

3

Bash Bish Falls
Tri-State Challenge

Salisbury—Lakeville—Taconic State Park
Bash Bish Falls State Forest
Mount Washington
South Egremont—Salisbury

The Tri-State Challenge is the longest and most difficult of the three rides based in Salisbury, Connecticut. It rolls around the southernmost, and one of the wildest, reaches of the Berkshire Range. A spectacular climb up the Bash Bish Falls gorge, a long stretch across a mountaintop ridge, and a fast descent of Mount Washington's eastern flank are among the highlights along the way.

Sections of this countryside seem from a half-century past. They have escaped the attention of the summer-home gentry that in many places nearby is displacing the bovine population. One reason may be that many of these roads are nearly impossible to find. They fall into the cracks between most Connecticut, New York, and Massachusetts state maps.

Several stretches of road on the New York side, fortunately or unfortunately depending on your view, have also escaped the attention of that state's paving crews. Come equipped with at least moderately rugged tires, and remember the words of Leif Thorne-Thomsen: "It's not a real New England ride without a little stretch of dirt road."

T-T, as he's known, was only half joking. As a former member of the U.S. amateur world championships team and the long-time cycling club coach of Lakeville's Hotchkiss School, he knows the value of this kind of ride in developing bike handling skills and stamina. Follow his suggestion and always ride rough or dirt roads with your elbows loose and relaxed, using your arms to absorb road vibration.

Not that this ride should appeal only to the most rugged riders. It offers spectacular scenery as well as a tough climb. Northerly views from Rudd Pond Road toward Bear Mountain—at over 2,300 feet Connecticut's highest— and the more distant Lion's Head and Mount Everett accompany the long rolling warmup stretch through farmland dotted with purple silos. And the final miles along Route 41 into Salisbury make up in smoothness for the several miles of rougher road on the opposite side of the range.

The climb through Bash Bish State Forest is accompanied by the sound of Bash Bish Brook plunging over 60-foot falls. From June to July, mountain laurel bloom on the narrow canyon's walls. The route rises approximately 1,000 feet in 5.4 miles to its highest point at the turnoff for Mount Everett Reservation. A mile-long downhill stretch, directly alongside Bash Bish Brook, divides the climb into two manageable sections. You may want to take a quick detour to the Depot Deli for a preclimb snack.

The town of Mount Washington, with fewer than fifty inhabitants, marks the climb's end. You'll know you're there when you reach the modest Church of Christ in Mount Washington, standing alone deep in the forest.

The Basics

Start: Salisbury, the most northwesterly town in Connecticut. From New York, follow Rte. 22 to Millerton, then turn east on Rte. 44 into Connecticut and through Lakeville to Salisbury. From Connecticut or Massachusetts, follow Rte. 7 to Canaan, then turn west onto Rte. 44 into Salisbury. Combined routes 44 and 41 become Main St. Park on either side or behind the new Town Hall at the town's southern end.

Length: 45.3 miles.

Terrain: Mountainous, featuring a 1,000-foot, 5.4-mile climb. Short stretches of rough or dirt road.

Food: The Depot Deli, at the entrance to Bash Bish Falls State Park, at 19.4 miles.

Miles & Directions

- 0.0 From Salisbury Town Hall, join combined routes 44W and 41S, here named Main St. toward Lakeville.
- 2.0 In Lakeville, bear right with Rte. 44W toward Millerton.
- 3.5 Stay right on Rte. 44 at intersection with Rte. 112.
- 4.4 Right on State Line Rd. This sharp turn is unmarked and easy to miss. It comes at the top of a rise just before the road enters New York State. State Line Rd. dips and sweeps left immediately.
- 5.0 Bear left at fork.
- 5.6 Right at first intersection onto Dutchess County Rte. 62, called Rudd Pond Rd., following signs toward Taconic State Park.
- 8.4 Straight through intersection with Kay Rd., as Rte. 62 turns into Rte. 63 but is still named Rudd Pond Rd.
- 11.1 Stay right with Rudd Pond Rd., passing turnoff for White Horse Crossing on left.
- 12.7 Right onto Under Mountain Rd., a well-maintained dirt road, at intersection with Altenburg Rd.
- 14.7 Right onto Rte. 22 as Under Mountain Rd. ends.
- 14.8 Take first possible right turn off Rte. 22, onto Weed Mine Rd., after just 50 yards.
- 17.4 Right onto unpaved Valley View Rd. at fork. This narrow lane soon curves to the right through a small farm and climbs a short hill. Watch out for the tractors and registered Holsteins.
- 18.9 Left with Valley View Rd. at intersection.

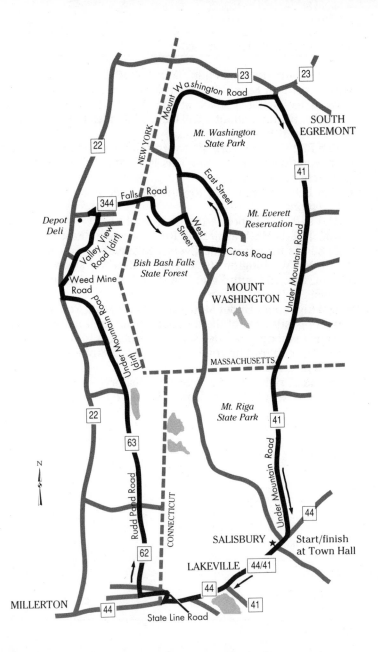

- 19.2 Valley View Rd. ends. Turn left at T.
- 19.4 Right on Falls Rd., Rte. 344. You may want to detour 50 yards to left for a snack at the Depot Deli. From here this route will climb about 1,000 feet in 5.4 miles to the turnoff for Mt. Everett Reservation.
- 22.8 Right at T, toward Mt. Everett Reservation and Salisbury, crossing over the stream. This is West St. Three very steep switchbacks follow.
- 23.9 Left on Cross St., toward Mt. Everett Reservation and Egremont.
- 24.5 Left at T opposite the Church of Christ in Mt. Washington. This is Mt. Washington Rd., also called East St.
- 24.8 Pass turnoff for Mt. Everett Reservation on right.
- 27.8 Mt. Washington Rd. begins to descend steeply, curving right, toward South Egremont. Continue on this road until it ends.
- 32.4 Right onto Under Mountain Rd., Rte. 41S. You are now on the opposite side of the mountain from the road of the same name earlier in the ride. South Egremont is to the left. Follow this smooth, rolling road for the next 12.8 miles back to Salisbury.
- 45.2 Bear right onto Main St. in Salisbury.
- 45.3 Arrive at Salisbury Town Hall on right.

Connecticut Seaport Classic

Center Groton—Mystic—Stonington
North Stonington—Clarks Falls
Preston City—Center Groton

One of the most popular club rides in Connecticut is the annual Seaport Metric Century, renamed here the Connecticut Seaport Classic, organized by the Pequot Cyclists. A metric century is a ride that covers 100 kilometers, or about 62 miles. This ride and the following Connecticut Seaport Ramble, a shorter 25-mile route, explore the state's southeastern corner from the historic seaport towns of Mystic and Stonington to the inland hills overlooking Long Island Sound.

In the club ride's most recent running, at the stroke of eight on a quiet Sunday morning, nearly a hundred cyclists rolled out of the parking lot of the Groton Schwinn Cyclery shop in Center Groton. Latecomers hurriedly pumped air into their tires and made their final mechanical adjustments before taking off after the pack. Many of the riders wore club jerseys identifying them as Sound Cyclists, Narragansett Bay Wheelmen from next door, or Charles River Wheelmen from farther north. Others favored the splashy jerseys of European professional teams.

One group drafted behind the double-powered pace of a tandem bicycle for the opening stretch through rolling orchards down to the Mystic River. Reaching the waterfront opposite historic Mystic Seaport with time to spare, all slowed to look across the river and admire the maritime museum village's nineteenth-century skyline of tall masts and rigging.

Following an inland excursion along the Pequot Trail, a road that evolved over the centuries from an Indian footpath, the ride turned back toward the ocean with a harborfront run into historic Stonington. Everyone's bikes bounced down a not quite reconstructed road to the docks for a view of distant Fisher's Island, a private vacation retreat.

Riding inland, north from Stonington, a series of gradual uphills led into the Seaport Classic's big climb, a long stretch from the woods to the open, rounded hilltops looking back toward Long Island Sound. The trellised grapevines of Crosswoods Vineyard mark the end of the climb. Halfway up, a group of racers on a training ride whipped by in a tight pace line, ten riders in a row, each drafting behind the man in front. They did not even slow for the view.

The Pequot Cyclists had set up a rest stop off Route 2 at the 36-mile mark, with stacks of donuts and coolers of juice, all financed by the modest registration fee. The riders regrouped here before setting out for the Classic's second half, which followed back roads winding through small farms and Yankee woodland towns.

Join the Pequot Cyclists for their next running of the Seaport Classic, usually held in May. Or organize your own group and follow the directions below. Because the route is mapped mostly along back roads, its many turns often follow in rapid succession. As most cycling clubs do for large, organized rides, the Pequot Cyclists paint arrows on the road to supplement the printed directions. These are a great help because they free you from the need to check the directions while riding. Look for the club's small but bright green arrows as you roll along.

The Basics

Start: Center Groton. Park at Groton Schwinn Cyclery on Rte. 184. To get there, take exit 88 off I-95 onto Rte. 117N. Turn right onto Rte. 184 for one-half mile. The shop will be on your left.
Length: 62.0 miles.

Terrain: Rolling coastal inlands. One long, gradual climb and several short ones. Many long, flat stretches along rivers and through farms.

Food: Many options in grocery and convenience stores along the way. Or pack a sandwich to eat at the Crosswoods Vineyard atop a hill with a view of distant Long Island Sound.

Miles & Directions

- 0.0 Ride east (away from Rte. 117 intersection) on Rte. 184.
- 0.9 Right on Flanders at top of short rise.
- 1.5 Left on Noank Ledyard Rd.; orchards on the left.
- 2.2 Left on Sandy Hollow Rd.
- 2.9 Cross Allyn St.
- 3.3 Left on High St.
- 3.4 Right on Rindloss St.
- 3.6 Right on River Rd.
- 4.2 Left on Starr St., then bear right into Pearl St.
- 4.5 Left on Eldridge St.
- 4.6 Right on Gravel St., which passes along the riverfront opposite Old Mystic Village.
- 4.8 Left on Main St., Rte. 1, through Mystic, crossing the iron grate drawbridge over the Mystic River.
- 6.8 Left on Cove Rd., 2 miles out of downtown Mystic.
- 8.1 Right on Mistuxet Ave., which then merges right into Jerry Browne Rd.
- 8.5 Left on Deans Mill Rd. This is an easy one to miss. It's the narrowest of the three choices and turns down toward the river. Deans Mill soon turns up from the river, becoming a single-lane road winding through a woods.
- 9.5 Right on the Pequot Trail.
- 10.3 Right on Flanders Rd.
- 11.5 Left as Flanders Rd. appears to end. The road sign says this is Deans Mill again, although maps show it as Flanders Rd. continued.
- 12.2 Cross Rte. 1 at stoplight. Cross river and follow signs into Stonington.

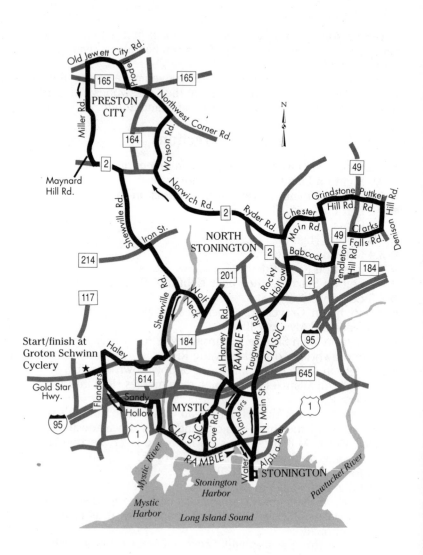

- 12.8 Left on Trumbull St.
- 12.9 Right on Alpha St., crossing the railroad tracks.
- 13.2 Left onto Water St., continuing straight through Stonington to its waterfront. When you reach the parking area jutting into the harbor, turn around and return along Water St.
- 13.5 Right onto Cannon Square.
- 13.6 Left on Main St.
- 14.1 Turn left, to circle Stonington Green.
- 14.2 Right, back onto Alpha St. and across the railroad tracks.
- 14.5 Left onto Trumbull St.
- 14.6 Right on North Main St.
- 15.3 Straight across Rte. 1.
- 16.9 Right on the Pequot Trail.
- 17.2 Continue straight; the Pequot Trail becomes Taugwonk Rd.
- 20.2 Right on Stony Brook Rd.
- 21.2 Straight across Rte. 184, Rocky Hollow Rd.
- 22.3 Cross Rte. 2.
- 22.5 Continue straight through North Stonington Center.
- 22.6 Right on Babcock Rd., at the top of this hill.
- 24.3 Left on Rte. 49.
- 25.6 Right on Rte. 216.
- 26.8 Left on Denison Hill Rd.
- 27.9 Left on Puttker Rd.
- 28.9 Cross Rte. 49.
- 30.9 Right on Chester Main Rd. Begin climb through vineyards. Be sure to look back at the top for a view over the rolling farmland and vineyards to the ocean.
- 32.9 Turn right on Wyassup Rd. at the bottom of the hill and then turn left immediately onto Ryder Rd.
- 34.5 Turn right onto Rte. 2. Ride to the right of the broad, clean shoulder. Climb gradually for the next mile, then enjoy a slight downhill for the following three.
- 38.2 Right onto Watson Rd.
- 39.8 Right on Hollowell Rd.
- 40.6 Left on Northwest Corner Rd., which passes between two century-old rows of oak trees and through a vast Christmas tree farm.

- 41.7 Continue across Rte. 164 in Preston.
- 42.0 Left on Rte. 165.
- 42.5 Right on Prodell Rd.
- 43.8 Left on Old Jewett City Rd.
- 45.1 Left on McLimon Rd.
- 45.8 Cross Rte. 165, continuing straight onto Miller Rd.
- 48.9 Left on Maynard Hill Rd., which follows the line of a north-south ridge, offering views to either side.
- 49.0 Left on Rte. 2.
- 50.1 Right on Shewville Rd.
- 53.2 Left onto Iron St.
- 53.3 Right back onto Shewville Rd.
- 55.5 Right with Shewville Rd. as Whitville Rd. turns left.
- 57.7 Right on Rte. 184, Gold Star Highway.
- 58.0 Right on Welles Rd.
- 58.4 Cross Rte. 184 and then Cow Hill Rd., continuing straight onto Packer Rd.
- 59.2 Left on Rte. 184.
- 59.8 Right on Haley Rd. at the flashing red light.
- 60.4 Left on Quaker Farm Rd.
- 60.5 Left on Lambtown Rd.
- 61.1 Right onto Rte. 184.
- 62.0 Ride ends back at Groton Schwinn Cyclery.

5

Connecticut Seaport Ramble

Center Groton—Mystic—Stonington
Center Groton

The Connecticut Seaport Ramble is modeled after a shorter ride offered by the Pequot Cyclists on the day of the club's annual Seaport Metric Century ride, presented on the preceding pages as the Connecticut Seaport Classic. The Ramble follows the same route as the Classic through the historic seaport towns of Mystic and Stonington. It then circles briefly inland to rejoin the tail end of the Classic's route for the trip back to their mutual starting point at the Groton Schwinn Cyclery shop in Center Groton.

Covering a distance of less than 30 miles with no major hills, this leisurely tour leaves plenty of time to explore the two historic seaport towns on its route. In Mystic, detour onto Route 27S to visit Mystic Seaport, a museum village that recreates everyday life in a nineteenth-century maritime community. Admission costs $10, but the view from Gravel Street across the river is free. Stonington is a very real, modern maritime community of restored colonial homes, tasteful shops, and docks for the sailing set. Take time to explore this pretty coastal village.

The Basics

Start: Center Groton. Park at Groton Schwinn Cyclery on Rte. 184. To get there, take exit 88 off I-95 onto Rte. 117N. Turn right

onto Rte. 184 for one-half mile. The shop will be on your left.
Length: 27.8 miles.
Terrain. Flat seacoast and rolling coastal inlands.
Food: Many options in both Mystic and Stonington, the tour's
two highlights.

Miles & Directions

- 0.0 Ride west (away from the Rte. 117 intersection) on Rte.
  184.
- 0.9 Right on Flanders at top of short rise.
- 1.5 Left on Noank Ledyard Rd.; orchards on the left.
- 2.2 Left on Sandy Hollow Rd.
- 2.9 Cross Allyn St.
- 3.3 Left on High St.
- 3.4 Right on Rindloss St.
- 3.6 Right on River Rd.
- 4.2 Left on Starr St., then bear right into Pearl St.
- 4.5 Left on Eldridge St.
- 4.6 Right on Gravel St., which passes along the riverfront
  opposite Old Mystic Village.
- 4.8 Left on Main St., Rte. 1, through Mystic, crossing the iron
  grate drawbridge over the Mystic River.
- 8.8 Right on North Water St. toward Stonington.
- 9.4 Left on Trumbull St.
- 9.5 Right on Alpha St., crossing the railroad tracks.
- 9.8 Left onto Water St., continuing straight through Stonington to its waterfront. When you reach the parking area jutting
  into the harbor, turn around and return along Water St.
- 10.1 Right onto Cannon Square.
- 10.2 Left on Main St.
- 10.7 Turn left, to circle Stonington Green.
- 10.8 Right, back onto Alpha St. and across the railroad tracks.
- 11.1 Left onto Trumbull St.
- 11.2 Right on North Main St.
- 11.9 Straight across Rte. 1.

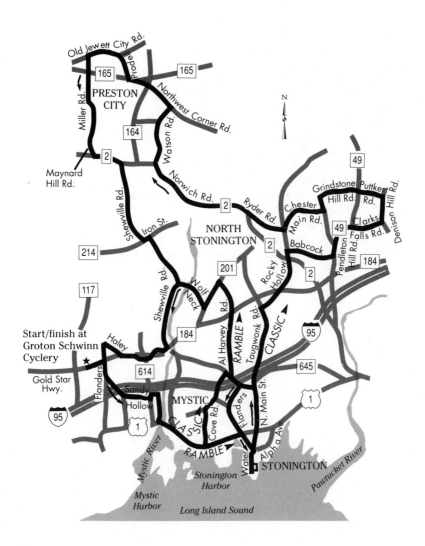

- 13.6 Left on the Pequot Trail.
- 14.8 Right on Al Harvey Rd.
- 17.3 Straight across Rte. 184.
- 18.7 Left on Rte. 201.
- 20.0 Right on Wolf Neck Rd.
- 21.0 Straight across Lantern Hill Rd.
- 21.5 Straight onto Shewville Rd.
- 23.5 Right onto Rte. 184.
- 23.8 Right on Welles Rd.
- 24.2 Cross Rte. 184 and then Cow Hill Rd., continuing straight onto Packer Rd.
- 25.0 Left on Rte. 184.
- 25.6 Right on Haley Rd. at the flashing red light.
- 26.2 Left on Quaker Farm Rd.
- 26.3 Left on Lambtown Rd.
- 26.9 Right onto Rte. 184.
- 27.8 Ride ends back at Groton Schwinn Cyclery.

6

Norwichtown Challenge

Norwichtown—Baltic—Hanover
North Windham—South Windham
North Franklin—Norwichtown

The Pequot Cyclists' John Fletcher enthusiastically recommends this 52-mile tour from Norwichtown to the woodlands of Windham County as one of the most rewarding rides in Connecticut. This is the state's undiscovered corner. Far off the state's principal tourist routes up the Housatonic River and along Long Island Sound, the Norwichtown Challenge explores the backwoods landscape between Norwich, an old industrial center, and Willimantic. The ride passes through Mohegan and Beaver Brook state forests, the southernmost of seven parklands spread across this part of the state.

The Pequot Cyclists pass this way every September, when the club hosts its annual century ride, of which this challenge is an abbreviated version. The longer ride extends all the way to the state's far northeastern corner. Both wind through a countryside of rivers and valleys, farms and small Yankee towns.

The Basics

Start: Norwichtown green, reached from exit 82 off Rte. 52 (Rte. 395) just north of Norwich.

Length: 54.0 miles.
Terrain: Hilly.
Food: Grocery and convenience stores.

Miles & Directions

- 0.0 From the Norwichtown green, turn right onto east Town St.
- 0.1 Left on Mediterranean Lane.
- 0.8 Right on Wightman Ave.
- 1.2 Right on Case St.
- 1.8 Left on Scotland Rd.
- 4.6 Right on Maple Ave. to Rte. 97.
- 4.7 Left on Rte. 97 to town of Baltic.
- 4.9 Turn right with Rte. 97 across the Shetucket River. Stay left with Rte. 97 on the other side.
- 5.5 Right on Main St., also called Baltic–Hanover Rd.
- 7.7 Right on Parkwood Rd. in Hanover.
- 9.5 Right on Woodchuck Hill Rd.
- 10.5 Continue straight across Water St.
- 11.7 Left on Lisbon Rd.
- 14.9 Right on Rte. 14.
- 15.5 Left on Kitt Rd.
- 16.6 Left on North Society Rd.
- 18.7 Continue straight on North Society Rd.
- 20.7 Left on Windham Rd.
- 22.2 Right on Raymond Rd.
- 24.4 Cross Rte. 97.
- 24.6 Right on Kemp Rd.
- 26.3 Right on Ziegler Rd.
- 28.4 Continue straight onto Chewink Rd.
- 28.5 Left on Lynch Rd.
- 29.9 Left on Rte. 6.
- 30.9 Left on Rte. 203 in North Windham. Follow Rte. 203 for the next 5.2 miles, crossing Rte. 14 midway.
- 36.1 Left on Rte. 32 through South Windham.

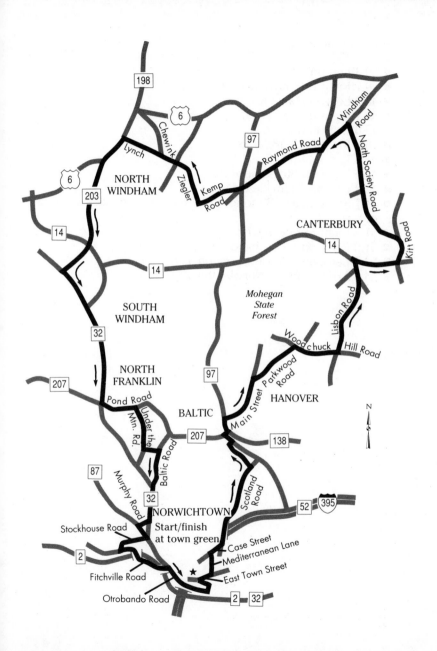

- 39.3 Left on Rte. 207 in North Franklin.
- 40.7 Right on Under the Mountain Rd.
- 42.3 Left on Plains Rd.
- 43.1 Right on Baltic Rd.
- 45.0 Left on Rte. 32.
- 45.6 Right on Murphy Rd.
- 46.3 Left on Rte. 87.
- 46.6 Right on Stockhouse Rd.
- 48.2 Left on Fitchville Rd.
- 51.7 Right on Rte. 32 to exit 27. Prepare for quick succession of turns.
- 51.8 Right onto exit 27 ramp.
- 51.9 Right onto Otrobando Ave.
- 53.7 Left onto the New London Turnpike.
- 54.0 Arrive back at Norwichtown green.

Maine

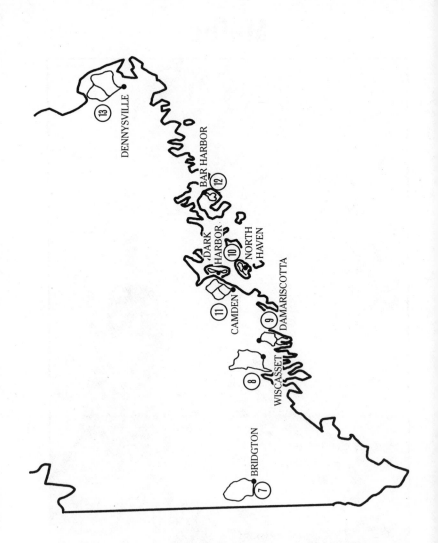

Maine

7

Moose Country Challenge

Bridgton—Lovell—Center Lovell—Lynchville
East Stoneham—Waterford—Bridgton

Celebrate the spring thaw by taking on the Moose Country Challenge, a 50-mile route that explores the pond-studded terrain between Sebago Lake and the White Mountains. On a sunny day in mid-March, this is the perfect ride from which to enjoy the scenes of a winter's end. You will see skiers enjoying the last runs of the season on the slopes of Pleasant Mountain. Snowmobiles will be roaring across the fields, zipping around widening patches of corn stubble. Ice fishermen will be dragging their bobhouses off of Moose Pond and every other body of water along the route.

The Moose Country Challenge will appeal to cyclists wanting to enjoy alpine views without suffering any more than a couple of short, steep climbs. This wilderness route is a favorite inland tour of Maine's largest cycling club, the Penobscot Wheelmen, at any time in the cycling season. This club also recommends the following Kennebec Crossing and Acadia Carriage Path tours as among the finest rides in New England.

Highlights of this trip include several pristine lakeside villages. Of these, Waterford is the standout. First settled in 1775, this congregation of white clapboard buildings appears to have changed little in the last 200 years. It is now a National Historic Site. Stop at the old L. R. Rounds General Store, recently renovated and reopened by Martha Eaton, who can fill you in on the town's history and its current goings-on.

Martha notes that the Penobscot Wheelmen aren't the only cyclists to have discovered Waterford. Several other groups tour through here regularly as well. One clan rides across the continent from Portland, Oregon, to Portland, Maine, every year, always stopping at her store. "They came over the Sweden Hills, just to the west of here," Martha reported, "and said they had come all the way across the country and not seen any climbs so hard." The following directions mercifully skirt those hills and provide a relatively flat return to Bridgton.

The Basics

Start: Bridgton, just northwest of Sebago Lake. From Portland, Maine, take Rte. 302W directly into Bridgton, turn left with Rte. 302 as Rte. 117 continues straight, and park at the top of the hill, near the granite memorial. Bridgton can also be reached easily from Conway, New Hampshire, via Rte. 302E.
Length: 50.0 miles.
Terrain: Surprisingly flat, considering the terrific views of mountains all around. Two climbs, just less than a mile long each: from North Waterford to Waterford, at 26.3 miles, and from North Bridgton to Highland Rd., at 37.0 miles.
Food: Try the L. R. Rounds General Store, on the left in Waterford at 30.8 miles. Lovell, East Stoneham, and Bridgton have their general stores also.

Miles & Directions

- 0.0 From the granite memorial in the center of Bridgton, ride west on Rte. 302, here called North High St., toward Sweden and Fryeburg.
- 1.2 Bear left with Rte. 302W toward Fryeburg, as Rte. 93 forks right toward Sweden.
- 5.5 Right on Knights Hill Rd., opposite the Pleasant Mountain ski area. Knights Hill Rd. passes through mostly unpopulated

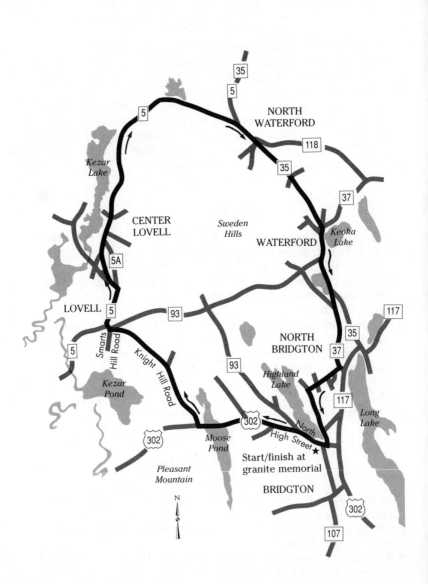

woods, climbing gradually for half of its 5.8 miles, then descending for the other half.

- 11.3 Left on Rte. 93, Lovell Rd., then bear right with the road into Lovell.
- 11.4 Right on Rte. 5N. There is a general store on the left in a hundred yards.
- 13.1 Stay with Rte. 5, following the sign toward Stoneham and Bethel, as Rte. 5A turns to the right.
- 13.5 Stay on Rte. 5, passing turnoff for Kezar Lake and The Narrows.
- 19.9 Pass through North Lovell on Rte. 5.
- 22.0 Keewaydin Lake on left.
- 23.9 Pass through East Stoneham. Country store on left. Rte. 5 straightens and flattens.
- 25.3 Arrive at the "international signpost" intersection. Continue straight onto Rte. 35S as Rte. 5N turns left.
- 26.3 Bear right and uphill at the fork, staying on Rte. 35S toward Waterford and Harrison. Rte. 118 bears left.
- 30.8 Right at bottom of hill into downtown Waterford. Rte. 35 merges into Rte. 37 here. L. R. Rounds General Store follows on the left. Town beach on Keoka Lake in another 100 yards.
- 32.2 Stay right with combined routes 35 and 37 as Sweden Rd. turns right.
- 33.7 Fork right with Rte. 37S toward Bridgton as Rte. 35 turns left toward Harrison. Bear Pond on right.
- 37.0 Enter North Bridgton and turn right, uphill on Chadbourne Hill Rd., which borders the grounds of Bridgton Academy.
- 38.5 Left at T, following big yellow arrow to the left. This is Highland Rd., although it is unmarked here.
- 40.9 Right at T, immediately following Highland Lake Park on the right. This is Rte. 302W, in downtown Bridgton.
- 50.0 Arrive at granite memorial at intersection of North and South High sts. in Bridgton.

8

Kennebec Crossing Challenge

Wiscasset—Whitefield—Gardiner—Richmond Days Ferry—Wiscasset

The Kennebec Crossing Challenge is an exhilarating tour around the thumb of land formed by the Sheepscot and Kennebec rivers as they rush down to the tangle of islands between Bath and Boothbay Harbor. Its 55 miles of rolling roads lead from the historic seafaring town of Wiscasset to more modest farming communities inland and the old mill town of Richmond before following the course of the Kennebec back to the sea.

The Penobscot Wheelmen's Ken Bell recommends this half century as a tour that avoids Maine's crowded coastal roads and offers a riverine landscape instead. Ken encourages out-of-staters to explore regions inland of Route 1, Maine's shoreline thoroughfare. Citing tourist traffic and the difficulty of mapping longer circular routes across country broken up by countless rivers and bays, he says simply that the coast is not the best place to ride.

Ken also suggests exploring this route in the months of September and October. This is the season when the weather turns crisp, brilliant leaves begin to rattle off their trees, and the season's crops of pumpkin and squash dot the acres of fields that slope toward the Kennebec. Keep an eye on the weather, though. Early northeasters, with gale warnings at sea and snow watches inland, do strike as early as Columbus Day weekend.

Be sure to stop and enjoy some of the sights along this rural route. Look for the Sheepscot Reversing Falls, reached by a short dirt-road detour to the right 4 miles into the ride. A collection of monumental abstract sculptures unexpectedly grace the roadside leading into Whitefield. Pack a sandwich to eat along the banks of the Kennebec River. And leave plenty of time to explore historic Wiscasset itself. The elegant homes of nineteenth-century merchants and captains still grace this former seafaring town. And along its waterfront lie the weathered remains of the last two four-masted clipper ships known to exist, reminders of an older Maine.

The Basics

Start: Wiscasset. From Rte. 95 north, take exit 22 toward Brunswick and Rte. 1. Follow Rte. 1 through Bath to Wiscasset. Park in Wiscasset town center.
Length: 55.2 miles.
Terrain: Rolling hills between two rivers. No major climbs.
Food: There are several coffee shops on Water St., Gardiner's main street, midway at 23.3 miles. Wiscasset offers a variety of small cafes and restaurants for a meal before or after the ride.

Miles & Directions

- 0.0 Follow Rte. 218N out of Wiscasset, passing the town's nineteenth-century Old Jail, on a rise overlooking the Sheepscot River.
- 5.9 Pass Alna's eighteenth-century Center School and Meeting House on left, continuing on 218N. Look back over your shoulder. There's a nice view toward the ocean from here.
- 12.9 Pass Whitefield Ring Cross sculpture, cut from a 20-foot granite cemetery stone, on right. Look for other abstract sculptures in clearing on left.

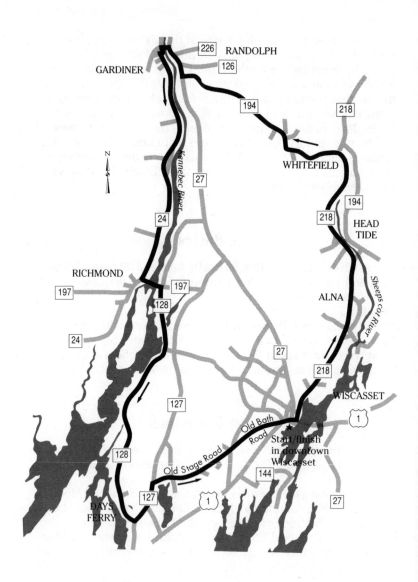

226 RANDOLPH
126
GARDINER
194
218

N

Kennebec River

27
WHITEFIELD
194
24
218 HEAD
TIDE
RICHMOND
197
197
128
ALNA
24
Sheepscot River
27
218
127
WISCASSET
1
Old Bath Road
128
★ Start/finish
in downtown
Wiscasset
Old Stage Road
144
127
1
27
DAYS
FERRY

- 13.2 Entering village of Whitefield, bear left on Rte. 194W toward Pittston. Rtes. 218 and 194E turn right on bridge across Sheepscot River. Rte. 194W traverses the rolling hills from the Sheepscot to the Kennebec River.
- 21.4 Right on Rte. 27N toward Randolph and Gardiner. Rte. 194 ends here.
- 22.7 Follow Rte. 27 as it turns left across bridge over Kennebec River and into Gardiner.
- 23.0 Immediate left onto Rte. 24, nearest river, coming off bridge.
- 23.3 Follow Rte. 24 as it takes a quick right into the town's shopping district. One block farther, at the stoplight, turn left with Rte. 24, here called Water St., to follow the Kennebec River south. Water St., both to the left and to the right of the light, is home to several casual lunch spots.
- 33.9 Following Rte. 24S from Gardiner, take a sharp left onto Rte. 197E, toward Dresden Mills, immediately after passing under railway tracks. You have missed this turn if you enter Richmond.
- 34.5 Rte. 197E crosses Kennebec River. Caution: Walk bike across slick iron grate bridge.
- 35.0 Right on Rte. 128S toward Woolwich.
- 45.9 Pass through Days Ferry, catching a glimpse of the Bath Iron Works downriver.
- 46.3 Left onto Rte. 127N at T. From here, this ride follows a series of back roads home to Wiscasset rather than joining the more direct but heavily trafficked Rte. 1.
- 48.3 Right onto Old Stage Rd. This turn is unmarked, but it is the second possible right off Rte. 127.
- 51.9 Right at fork after passing cemetery on left.
- 53.4 At stop sign, turn left on Old Bath Rd., which is also unmarked.
- 54.8 Left onto Rte. 1N for final stretch into Wiscasset. Watch out for traffic along this busy stretch of road.
- 55.2 Arrive in Wiscasset town center.

9

Pemaquid Point Cruise

Damariscotta—Round Pond—New Harbor—
Pemaquid Point
South Bristol—Damariscotta

Centuries ago, glaciers carved out the rocky shoreline that distinguishes Maine's coast from that of the Atlantic seaboard farther south. Midcoast, between Brunswick and Belfast, the glaciers scooped out a series of distinct peninsulas reaching south into the ocean. One of these, the finger of land from Damariscotta to Pemaquid Point, offers excellent cycling.

Maine Coast Cyclers, the leading purveyor of cycling vacations in the Down East state, recommends this circular route for its distinctly old salt flavor. It passes through traditional coastal villages where fishing is still a way of life, one that now coexists in harmony with a growing tourism industry. A lobster lunch, a lighthouse, spectacular ocean views, a sandy beach, and historical sites will beckon you to stop often enough that this 39-mile ride, with a longer option or several possible shortcuts, becomes an all-day outing.

From Damariscotta to Muscongus Bay, the road crossing the peninsula's top passes by four ponds. Red-winged blackbirds, perched atop reeds, survey the land while swaying in the wind. In Round Pond, detour to the left for a quick visit to the town's crowded and picturesque harbor.

As you ride south from Round Pond, Route 32 turns inland through woods before reaching the water again at Long Cove.

The tide often leaves colorful dinghys grounded on this little inlet's gravelly bottom. The road continues directly along the coast, passing the neat gardens of renovated clapboard homes, to New Harbor.

If you have been promising yourself a lobster feast, the Small Brothers restaurant in New Harbor is just the place. This casual lunch and dinner place is perched atop a wharf overlooking the town's active harbor. You can select the lobster you want boiled and then eat it on the deck, pausing to watch the comings and goings of the boats below.

From New Harbor it is only a short stretch south to Pemaquid Point. The lighthouse here stands sentinel over a series of ledges, striped with black and white rock, that march into the sea. Exploring them will give you a chance to digest that lunch. Also visit the small Fishermen's Museum inside the lighthouse itself.

Backtracking to New Harbor, the Pemaquid Point Cruise turns left to Pemaquid Beach, a beautiful crescent-shaped stretch of sand. There are a parking lot, snack bar, and facilities here. Nearby Colonial Pemaquid, the excavated foundations of an old settlement, provides evidence that this peninsula was colonized as a station for European fishermen as early as the sixteenth century.

From Pemaquid Beach the route winds up the peninsula's western flank back to Damariscotta. If you have extra time and energy, take the 15-mile round trip detour down to Christmas Cove. Named by Captain John Smith, who spent a lonely Christmas Eve here while exploring the coast in 1614, Christmas Cove is located on a tiny island connected to the mainland by a short drawbridge.

The Pemaquid Point Cruise is a good ride for even the beginning cyclist, as long as he or she is in shape. The many scenic spots will encourage everybody to stop, rest, and explore along the way. The Kennebec Crossing Challenge, a favorite ride of the Penobscot Wheelmen, explores the riverine inland north of Wiscasset, the next town south on Route 1; it makes a good companion ride. Combine the two tours for a full weekend of cycling.

The Basics

Start: Damariscotta, located on Rte. 1B about 28 miles east of Bath. Park in the public lot in the center of town, on the south side of the road behind a row of stores and offices.
Length: 38.9 or 53.9 miles.
Terrain: Gently rolling coastal terrain with several short hills.
Food: Every town on this route has at least one grocery store or snack bar. For a lobster lunch, stop at the Small Brothers wharf in New Harbor at 17.2 miles.

Miles & Directions

- 0.0 Leaving the Damariscotta parking lot, turn right onto Rte. 1BN. Continue straight as Rte. 129 turns south.
- 1.2 Right on Damariscotta Rd. toward Round Pond. Stay on this smooth road as several back routes take off to either side. Halfway along, you will skirt the northern tip of Biscay Pond.
- 6.4 Right on Rte. 32, continuing toward Round Pond.
- 10.7 Continue straight through Round Pond, a small lobster port, on Rte. 32. Detour to the left for a visit to the busy, compact harbor.
- 17.2 Entering New Harbor, turn left onto Rte. 130 toward Pemaquid Point.
- 20.0 Bear left with the main road to the lighthouse. When you reach the lighthouse, take the time to explore its rocky surroundings down to the water. Then backtrack on Rte. 130 toward New Harbor.
- 22. 6 Just before reaching the junction of rtes. 130 and 32, turn left down an unmarked road to Pemaquid Beach.
- 23.6 Right at intersection after passing Pemaquid Beach on the left. Or detour straight to see the Colonial Pemaquid restoration, unearthed foundations of a sixteenth- and seventeenth-century village with a small museum housing artifacts.

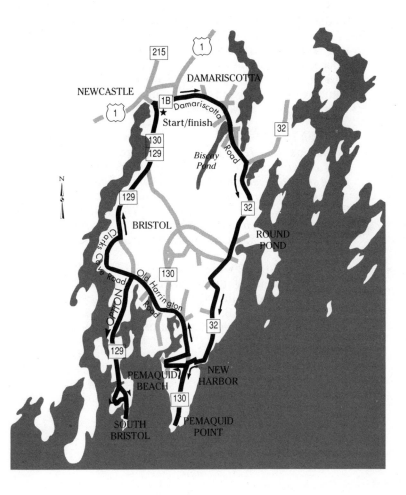

- 24.7 Left onto Rte. 130.
- 26.5 Left onto Old Harrington Rd., toward West Bristol, immediately after Rte. 130 crosses Pemaquid River.
- 27.5 Bear right with Old Harrington Rd. as Harbor Rd. turns left. You will pass the eighteenth-century Harrington Meeting House, and then the road changes its name to Pemaquid Rd.
- 29.5 Straight across Rte. 129 onto Clarks Cove Rd., which climbs briefly, descends to a small cove, and climbs again. This road leads back to Rte. 129 further north.

Turn left on Rte. 129 for a scenic detour that adds 15 miles to the ride. Rte. 129 travels down a narrow finger of land, over a drawbridge at 5 miles, and into South Bristol. Continue straight over the hill on Rte. 129 until the road turns to dirt just past Christmas Cove. As you return, circle around West Side Rd. to the left for 1.5 miles. This will put you back on Rte. 129, which will lead you back to the junction with Clarks Cove Rd. Continue with the directions below.

- 32.3 Left on Rte. 129, the final stretch back to Damariscotta.
- 35.7 Continue straight onto combined routes 129 and 130 as Rte. 130 joins from the right.
- 38.7 Left onto Rte. 1B.
- 38.9 Return to public parking lot on left in Damariscotta.

10

Two Penobscot Island Rambles

Penobscot Bay, that broad gap in the middle of the Maine coastline's smile, is dotted with dozens of islands. Many are no more than ocean-bound rock ledges, firm footing on rough seas for colonies of gulls, puffins, and other saltwater birds. Others are large enough for sizeable human populations to call them year-round homes.

Regular cyclists of Maine's coast agree that of all these islands, Islesboro and North Haven offer the best possibilities for cycling. Both are accessible by ferry from the mainland. The Islesboro Ramble, reached by regular ferry from Lincolnville, may be ridden on its own or as an extension of the Camden Hills Cruise. The North Haven Ramble involves a pleasant hour-long ferry ride from the modern seaport of Rockland, one of the largest lobster exporting centers in the world. The ferry passes the Rockland lighthouse, perched on the tip of a mile-long breakwater, on its way to the adjacent islands of North Haven and Vinalhaven.

Consider the rides mapped here more scenic excursions than serious training circuits. Islesboro offers the longer rides—20 or 28 miles, compared to the 11- and 21-mile routes on North Haven.

Each island is a quiet retreat at sea. Traffic is virtually non-existent. Narrow roads crisscross from one shore and one view to another. The well-kept homes of summer visitors and year-round residents sit interspersed among the woods, fields, bogs, and myriad coves.

On Islesboro, the Grindle Point Light, built in 1875, greets arriving ferry passengers. The free Sailor's Memorial Museum, near the ferry landing, is worth a visit at the ride's end if you have time before the ferry returns. On Pendleton Point, the island's southern tip, sunning rocks and picnic tables offer a chance to sit and enjoy the views.

On North Haven take the time to explore some of the side roads leading to the shore. A dirt road turning right off South Shore Road leads to the seaside Mullen Head State Park, a quiet spot for a picnic. A second side trip leads to Bartlett Harbor, a small sunning cove with a view back toward Rockland.

No matter which island you choose, you will find that these tide-bound outposts, whether shrouded in a morning fog or bathed by the sun, provide a welcome break from the mainland's more hurried pace.

Islesboro Ramble

Grindle Point—Dark Harbor
Pendleton Point—Islesboro
Turtle Head—Islesboro—Grindle Point

The Basics

Start: Grindle Point ferry landing, Islesboro. The ferry provides regular service between Grindle Point and Lincolnville, on the mainland's Rte. 1.
Length: 19.6 or 28.1 miles.
Terrain: Flat coastal roads with a few short dirt stretches.
Food: There are several potential lunch stops, including an ice cream shop, in the town of Dark Harbor at 3.1 miles on the longer option. Farther into the ride, at 7.0 or 15.5 miles, Durkee's General Store offers snack items.

Miles & Directions

- 0.0 Go straight after departing the ferry. (It's the only road.)
- 1.1 Turn right on West Side Rd. toward Dark Harbor.
- 2.1 Turn right at the T, onto Main Rd., toward Dark Harbor if you are riding the full 28.1-mile tour.

For a shorter, 19.6-mile circuit, turn left here instead and skip to mile 10.6 below. You'll ride only the northern end of the island, but it has the best views.

- 3.1 Arrive in town of Dark Harbor. There are a general store and an ice cream shop here. Continue straight through town.

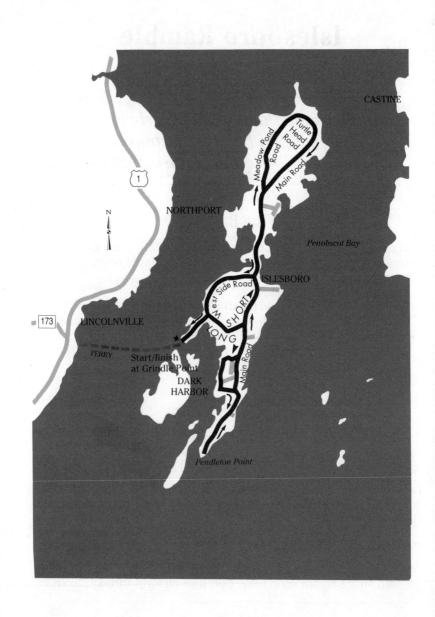

- 5.5 Arrive at Pendleton Point shortly after the road turns to dirt. There is a small beach here. From here, turn around and ride back toward Dark Harbor on Main Rd.
- 7.7 Turn left, two-tenths of a mile shy of the earlier ice cream stop. You should pass the Blue Heron restaurant on your right after the turn.
- 8.0 Stay right.
- 8.2 Continue straight through the intersection.
- 9.5 Turn left at the T, back onto Main Rd., a mile after passing the Islesboro Inn.
- 10.6 Continue straight as West Side Rd. joins from the left. Those riding the shorter option pick up the directions from here.
- 11.7 Turn right just past the small baseball field for a scenic detour.
- 12.3 Turn around where this turns into a private road.
- 12.9 Turn right, continuing northward on Main Rd.
- 13.1 Stay to the right, passing the Islesboro Historical Society on the left. You are now traversing the narrow piece of land linking Islesboro's northern and southern halves.
- 15.9 Bear left at the fork a half mile beyond Durkee's General Store. This is Meadow Pond Rd. Follow it as it loops around the island's northern end, turning into Turtle Head Rd. and then Main Rd. again.
- 22.0 Turn left, returning to Islesboro along Main Rd.
- 24.8 Turn right onto West Side Rd. just past the Islesboro Historical Society.
- 27.0 Turn right onto Ferry Rd.
- 28.1 Arrive back at ferry landing.

North Haven Ramble

North Haven—Mullen Head State Park
Pulpit Harbor
Bartlett Harbor—North Haven

The Basics

Start: The ferry landing in the town of North Haven on North Haven Island. The state of Maine provides regular ferry service between Rockland, on Rte. 1 and the mainland, and the island.
Length: 11.1 or 19.7 miles.
Terrain: Relatively flat coastal roads, with some stretches of rough or dirt road.
Food: There are general stores in North Haven, at the ride's beginning and end, and in Pulpit Harbor midway.

Miles & Directions

- 0.0 Disembark from ferry in town of North Haven and ride up Main St., passing the post office and general store, as Main St. curves uphill and to the right.
- 1.5 Bear right onto South Shore Rd., which, as with most roads on North Haven, may be unmarked. Follow this paved road all the way around the eastern end of the island and back toward Pulpit Harbor.
- 4.8 Stay on South Shore Rd., which changes to North Shore Rd. as it passes the intersection with Middle Rd.
- 8.7 Arrive in Pulpit Harbor and turn left across bridge. Bear right on other side.

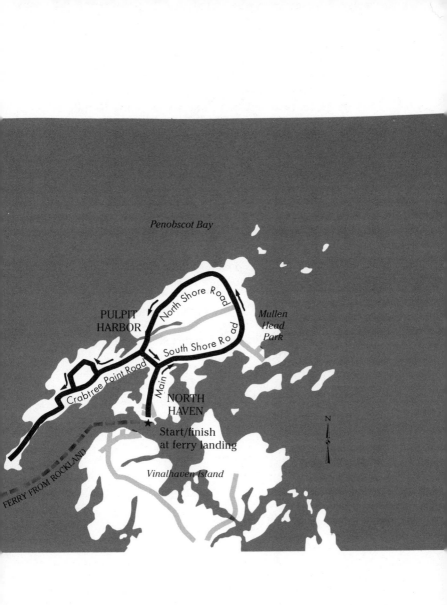

Penobscot Bay

PULPIT
HARBOR

North Shore Road

South Shore Road

Mullen
Head
Park

Crabtree Point Road

Main

NORTH
HAVEN

★ Start/finish
at ferry landing

Vinalhaven Island

FERRY FROM ROCKLAND

N

- 9.1 Right onto Crabtree Point Rd., probably unmarked, opposite the Grange Hall after passing the Pulpit Harbor Inn. For a shorter ride, bear left here instead, skipping to mile 17.7 in the directions below.
- 10.5 Turn right at the fork as you ride downhill between two meadows. An easy turn to miss, this is the first paved right turn off Crabtree Point Rd.
- 10.8 Turn left. The pavement gives way to a half-mile stretch of rough dirt road, whose condition is made up for by its views toward the mainland.

You may take an optional detour at 11.7 miles where, halfway down a steep hill, an unmarked right turn leads to Bartlett Harbor. This is a nice little cove for sunning. Return to the main road and go right to continue.

- 11.9 Turn right at the T. You have returned to Crabtree Point Rd., which continues toward the island's eastern end.
- 13.7 Crabtree Point Rd. turns to dirt shortly beyond the rocky beach on your right. From here, turn around and follow the main road all the way back to the center of the island.
- 17.7 Turn right at the T by the Grange Hall.
- 18.2 Bear right onto Main St. leading into North Haven.
- 19.7 Arrive back at ferry terminal.

11

Camden Hills Cruise

Camden—Lincolnville Center
Dog Island Corner—Northport
Lincolnville—Camden

One long loop with two shortcuts, the Camden Hills Cruise skirts Camden Hills State Park before entering an inland of rolling green hills, farms, and small ponds. Look for the 800-foot Maiden Cliff opposite the Lake Megunticook boat launch site on Route 52.

All three options pass the entrance to Camden Hills State Park, off Route 1 just over a mile north of Camden, in their final stretch. If you have any energy left, climb the park's toll road to the Mount Battie lookout tower. This mile-long, 600-foot ascent ends at an exposed summit offering views of Camden, the harbor, the coast, and Lake Megunticook.

Or, for a hike-and-bike weekend, return to the park the day after your ride. You will have a choice of three mountains, each with a choice of trails, to climb. Bald Rock Mountain offers exceptional views of Mount Desert and the Penobscot Bay islands. Mount Megunticook, the highest of the three, has a wooded summit but several lookouts from exposed ledges. Mount Battie's summit, reachable by foot or wheel, is the best-known viewpoint in the Camden Hills. A map and guide to the park's network of trails is supplied at the park entrance on Route 1.

If you would rather stay on your bike, visit one of the three nearby islands for a daylong exploration. Islesboro is accessible via ferry from Lincolnville, 6 miles north of Camden. North Haven and Vinalhaven can be reached by ferry from Rockland, 7 miles south of Camden. Of these three, Islesboro and North Haven offer the best cycling, as described earlier.

The Camden Hills Cruise and the two Penobscot Island Rambles are both favorite rides of Dennis and Ellen Curran, founders of the Maine Coast Cyclers inn-to-inn touring company. Both are experts at selecting ideal cycling routes, as they lead more than 360 riders, ranging from novice to experienced, on several dozen tours every year. The Currans have made their home in Camden, one of Maine's most popular sailing centers. They ride variations of this Camden Hills tour both on their own and as part of their company's cycling vacations.

The Basics

Start: Camden, 62 miles north of Brunswick on Rte. 1. Distances for this triple-option ride are measured from the flashing traffic light in Camden center.
Length: 19.8, 32.0, or 41.4 miles.
Terrain: Rolling hills; no exceptionally difficult climbs.
Food: Camden itself offers the greatest variety of places to eat along these routes. Nanny's corner store, midway on the longest option, is a welcome spot to sit and snack. Other choices abound along Rte. 1.

Miles & Directions

- 0.0 From the center of Camden on Rte. 1, ride northwest on Rte. 105, Washington St.
- 1.7 Right, uphill, onto Molyneux Rd. This may be unmarked. It is the first paved right turn following the pond on your right.
- 3.3 Sharp left soon after crossing the concrete bridge.

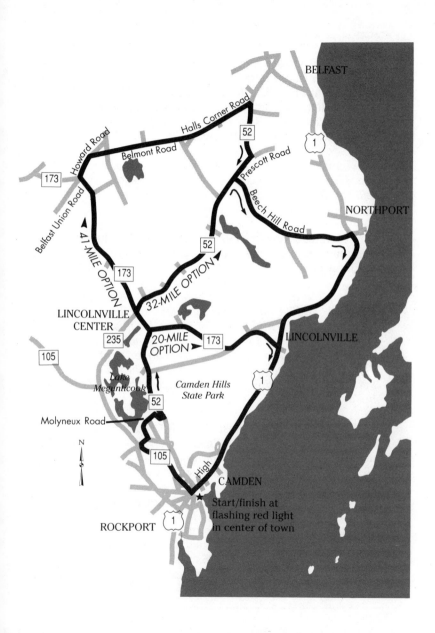

- 4.1 Stay left toward Megunticook Lake Beach, which follows in just over half a mile.
- 5.0 Left onto Rte. 52 after the lake.
- 6.9 Bear left, staying on Rte. 52, at the Youngstown Inn.
- 8.5 Turn left onto Rte. 173N toward Lincolnville Center if riding either of the two longer options.

To complete the shorter, 19.8-mile option, turn right onto Rte. 173S, toward Lincolnville and the Islesboro Ferry. You will reach Rte. 1 at 13.6 miles. Turn right and follow Rte. 1 south for the final 6.2 miles into Camden.

- 9.3 At intersection of routes 173 and 52 in Lincolnville Center, continue straight—and uphill—on Rte. 173N to continue with the longest option.

To complete the middle, 32.0-mile option, turn right onto Rte. 52N. At 15.4 miles, after 6 miles of rolling hills, turn right onto Beech Hill Rd. The only sign for this turn may be posted on a tree and visible to traffic coming from the opposite direction. Ride just a few yards ahead to check it out. (The longest Camden Hills option approaches this turn from the opposite direction.) From here, pick up the directions below at 25.2 miles.

- 14.9 Right at T onto Belfast Union Rd., leaving Rte. 173.
- 15.7 Right at fork onto Belmont Rd., although this is unmarked. There should be a farmhouse on your left.
- 16.4 Straight through the intersection marked by a school on your left.
- 19.5 Stay left. You are now on Halls Corner Rd.
- 20.8 Straight through intersection.
- 22.1 Right onto Rte. 52S. This intersection, officially Dog Island Corner, is marked by Nanny's Corner Store.
- 24.1 Right, staying on Rte. 52S.
- 25.2 Left onto Beech Hill Rd. Sometimes there is a sign on a tree marking this turn.

- 27.9 Stay left on Beech Hill as Knights Pond Rd. turns right. Then stay right soon after as another road turns off to the left.
- 30.0 Right onto Rte. 1S in Northport.
- 35.2 Pass through Lincolnville on Rte. 1S. The shortest ride joins here from the right on Rte. 173.
- 41.4 Arrive at flashing light in Camden center.

12

Acadia Carriage Path Cruise

Wally Bugbee, a ride leader for the Penobscot Wheelmen, wrote an article for his club's newsletter relating the trials of waiting out a Down East spring and the joys of finally getting out on a bicycle once again. Once you have taken this cruise, you will know why Wally and other club members look forward so eagerly to each year's first mountain bike tour of the carriage paths lacing Acadia National Park, on Maine's Mount Desert Island.

These dirt roads, winding through the island's interior forests and skirting its lakes and mountains, are one of Acadia's unique features. John D. Rockefeller, Jr., financed and directed their construction following World War I, between 1917 and 1933. The roads are superbly engineered, with gentle grades, stone culverts, and retaining walls. They cross sixteen stone bridges, each one individually and gracefully designed. Altogether, the park boasts 170 miles of trails and bridle and carriage paths.

Wally Bugbee guarantees that this is as beautiful and unusual a tour on a sunny afternoon as it is on a dark and dripping early morning in early April, when Acadia's forests and mountains take on an isolated magnificence most tourists miss. Highlights of the ride include spruce-framed views of Somes Sound and a dramatic passage along a ridge between Jordan Pond and the cliffs on Penobscot Mountain.

The Acadia Carriage Path Cruise covers nearly 30 miles of trails, most of which are navigable by mountain bike only. Although these broad paths are even and packed, there may be some loose spots. So take it easy, especially on downhill runs, and share the roads respectfully with joggers and horseback riders. The maze of carriage roads can be confusing; you may want to pick up a map at the Visitor Center to supplement the one here.

The Basics

Start: Park at the north end of the lot at the Acadia National Park Visitor Center, on Rte. 3 just north of Bar Harbor. The center itself is open only from mid-June through August.
Length: 27.7 miles.
Terrain: Hard-packed gravel and dirt roads, about half of which are graded specifically for bicycles. Several long but gradual climbs and descents.
Food: Be sure to pack a picnic lunch to enjoy at any of the numerous scenic spots along this backwoods tour. You'll be hungry; this is an energetic ride, and you should plan on devoting four to six hours to the tour to do it justice. The ride passes Jordan Pond House, a sit-down restaurant operated by the National Park Service, at 18.4 miles.

Miles & Directions

- 0.0 Follow the path away from the parking lot for half a mile to the end. This is uphill, with some steep pitches. But don't get discouraged; this is the worst hill on the ride.
- 0.5 Left for nine-tenths of a mile to the first left. There is a nice view from the top of the hill, with Frenchman Bay in the distance.
- 1.4 Left, following the sign for Bar Harbor, Eagle Lake, and Duck Brook. Go 1 mile to the next road on the left, which crosses a stone bridge high above a brook.
- 2.4 Bear right and continue for 1 mile to a fork.
- 3.4 Bear left, following the sign for Eagle Lake and Seal Harbor, and continue to a stone bridge underpass.

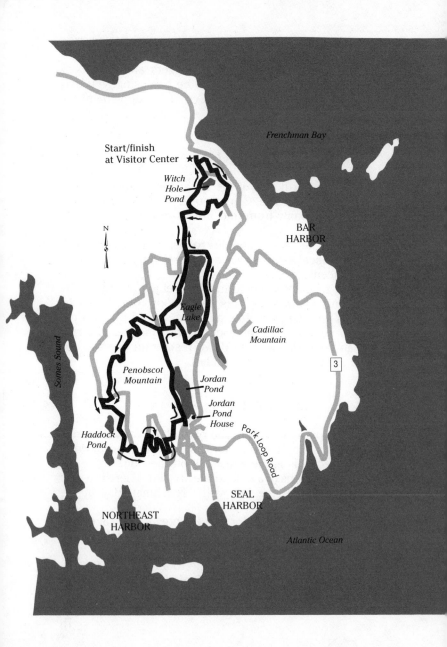

Start/finish at Visitor Center

Witch Hole Pond

Frenchman Bay

BAR HARBOR

N

Eagle Lake

Cadillac Mountain

3

Somes Sound

Penobscot Mountain

Jordan Pond

Jordan Pond House

Haddock Pond

Park Loop Road

SEAL HARBOR

NORTHEAST HARBOR

Atlantic Ocean

- 4.5 After passing beneath the stone bridge, continue straight to a small road on the right.
- 6.8 Turn right and ride to a crossroads.
- 7.0 Take the middle road, following the sign for "Around Mt.," and ride 5 miles to the next turn. This path climbs steadily for about 2 miles. There are many beautiful views along the way, including a fine vista of Somes Sound. Then enjoy the long descent.
- 12.0 Turn right and continue to the next fork.
- 12.3 Bear left toward Haddock Pond.
- 13.9 Turn left for just a short distance, then take the next right.
- 15.2 Turn right and go to an intersection with a gravel road on the left and a grass road on the right.
- 16.5 Turn left on the gravel road and go sharply uphill for six-tenths of a mile.
- 17.1 Take a sharp right, following the sign for Jordan Pond House, and continue to the next intersection.
- 18.4 Turn left, riding to the crossroads at Eagle Lake. This road passes high above Jordan Pond to the right and beneath the cliffs of Penobscot Mountain on the left. You may want to visit the Jordan Pond House, a short distance to the right, before making this turn.
- 20.9 Turn right.
- 21.1 Turn right and follow the broad road around Eagle Lake, returning to the stone bridge underpass you passed through earlier.
- 24.9 Pass beneath the bridge and continue to a T.
- 26.0 Turn left, following the sign for Witch Hole Pond on Paradise Hill.
- 27.0 Keep left, following signs for Paradise Hill and Hulls Cove, until you reach a narrow path on the left.
- 27.2 Turn left for the final descent to the Visitor Center parking lot.
- 27.7 Return to the Visitor Center.

Sunrise County Challenge

Dennysville—Pembroke—Perry—Baring
Moosehorn National Wildlife Refuge
West Pembroke—Dennysville

Maine's "Sunrise County" is a remote and unspoiled land of quiet natural beauty. Located at Maine's—and the U.S.A.'s—easternmost tip, this part of the state captures the spirit of the words Down East. Along its coastline, washed by the highest tides in the country, lie small fishing villages that rarely see visitors. Just inland lie pristine forests, clear lakes, and thousands of acres of wild blueberry fields. Washington County, the region's official name, is an ideal place for carefree cycling. Traffic is never heavy, and this section of the coast is not very hilly.

Credit for the Sunrise County Challenge goes to Dennis and Ellen Curran, founders of Maine Coast Cyclers, which offers inn-to-inn cycling vacations from Freeport, Maine, to Prince Edward Island, Canada. For those not wishing to travel this far east, the Currans have also contributed this chapter's Camden Hills Cruise and Penobscot Islands Rambles. Maine Coast Cyclers covers this route on one day of its five-day Sunrise County vacation.

This circuit starts out relatively flat, winding through a landscape of blueberry fields, lakes, and sea. It begins to roll on the road toward the Moosehorn National Wildlife Refuge, after you've had a chance to refresh yourself with a swim at Round

Lake's sandy beach. The final 10-mile stretch along Route 214 features the most hills. These, though, provide splendid views east toward the islands of Cobscook Bay.

The Basics

Start: The Lincoln House Inn in Dennysville. Dennysville is located approximately 115 miles east of Belfast along the easternmost section of Rte. 1. Turn west onto Rte. 86 for a short distance to reach the Lincoln House Inn.
Length: 43.6 or 65.3 miles.
Terrain: Moderately rolling coastal and inland wilderness.
Food: The Farmer's Union General Store at 16.4 miles and Dot's Lunch Stand at 20.1 miles are but two of several snack options along this route.

Miles & Directions

- 0.0 Ride east on Rte. 86 from the Lincoln House Inn in Dennysville, then turn left onto Rte. 1 north.
- 5.8 Left off Rte. 1 just before the Crossroads Motel, then bear left again. You should soon pass a church on the left.
- 8.4 Right across bridge and bear left on the other side.
- 10.1 Right at the first crossroads.
- 15.8 Bear right.
- 16.4 Left at T onto Rte. 1 north. You are in the town of Perry. The Farmer's Union General Store and Exxon station here make this a good place to break for a snack.
- 16.7 Right off Rte. 1 just in front of the Wigwam Store. This back road will take you along the shore.
- 16.9 Stay left, going uphill, at the fork. A detour to the right will lead you to a small ocean beach at Gleeson Point.
- 18.0 Enjoy the views of New Brunswick, Canada, along this downhill stretch.

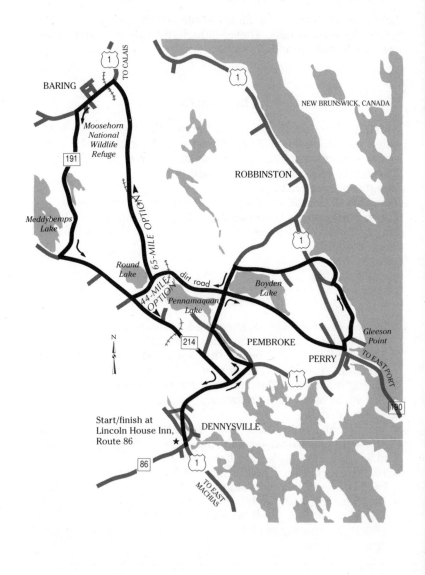

- 20.1 Right, following the small sign toward the Sunrise Shores Campground. Dot's Lunch Stand is just after the turn.
- 22.5 Cross Rte. 1.
- 26.1 Left at T. In a half mile, on Boyden Lake, there is a boat launch and swimming area.
- 27.3 Right onto dirt road at same crossroads you approached from opposite direction at 10.1 miles. This road will turn to pavement in just over a mile.
- 31.4 Right at T toward Moosehorn National Wildlife Refuge.

  You may cut off this ride's 23.1-mile northern loop by turning left here, turning left again onto Rte. 214 in 1.3 miles, then picking up the directions at mile 54.5.

- 32.1 Round Lake swimming beach—the nicest spot for a dip along this ride.
- 38.7 Moosehorn National Wildlife Refuge headquarters. Clean public rest rooms.
- 41.1 Left at T onto Rte. 1N.
- 43.5 Left off Rte. 1 onto Rte. 191S toward Machias.
- 50.6 Left onto Rte. 214E at T.
- 54.5 Shortcut joins longer circuit at this crossroads, with the Charlotte Town Hall on the right and Hatton's Grocery soon after.
- 60.7 Right onto Rte. 1 south at T.
- 65.2 Right onto Rte. 86 in Dennysville.
- 65.3 Arrive at Lincoln House Inn.

Massachusetts

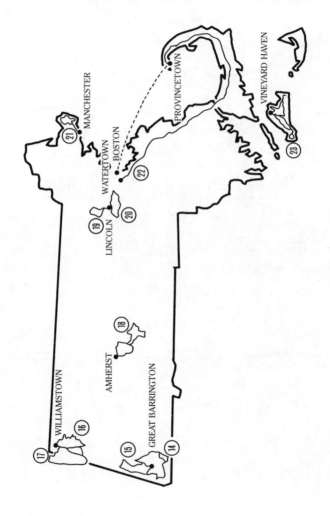

Massachusetts

14

Monument Valley Ramble

Great Barrington—South Egremont
Sheffield—Mill River
Monument Mountain—Great Barrington

The Monument Valley Ramble and Great Barrington Josh Billings Cruise are companion rides; each starts and ends at the Chamber of Commerce information booth in Great Barrington. Ride one on Saturday and one on Sunday to experience a weekend of classic Berkshire countryside. Or string them together to create one 60-mile figure-eight loop around the most bikeable corner of Massachusetts.

Both rides center on the Housatonic River's valley, winding across its plain and rolling along the foothills to either side. The Monument Valley Ramble, once you climb the mile-long hill at its very beginning, is virtually flat for its entire first half. The long stretch to Sheffield from the village of South Egremont, with the historic Egremont Inn at its center, is particularly easy cycling. This road passes country cottages, flat fields of corn, and even a herd of llamas.

Sheffield provides a perfect setting for a leisurely midway stop. This was the first town chartered in the Berkshires. Today it is a center for the region's antiques trade. Traffic on Route 7, Sheffield's Main Street, comes to a complete stop for almost an hour every Memorial Day, when the town celebrates with a fine local parade.

From Sheffield, the Monument Valley Ramble crosses the Housatonic on a new concrete bridge that in 1988 replaced a covered bridge ruined several years earlier by a too-heavy truck. At least the new bridge affords a midriver view down the valley toward Connecticut.

Once across the river, you can choose either of two routes leading to the top of the valley's eastern ridge. The shorter option follows County Road, which climbs gradually and in several steps alongside Ironwork Brook. The longer option adds 5 miles and climbs more steeply up a hillside rift cut by the Konkapot River. Both then rejoin for the ridgeside roll along Lake Buel and Monument Valley Roads back to Barrington.

Monument Mountain marks this tour's northern reach. The views of its pinkish rocky face from Monument Valley Road are a highlight of the tour. (Return without your bike for a hike to Monument Mountain's 1,700-foot peak, a longtime favorite local outing.) Ride the final stretch along Route 7 with caution as it careens downhill to Great Barrington.

Flat stretches across open farmland, a long but gradual climb, and gently rolling woodland roads combine to make the Monument Valley Ramble an ideal circuit for the rider wanting to progress beyond 20-mile loops. The more experienced rider, by tackling the hills aggressively and perhaps practicing sprints on the flats, will also find this a rewarding tour.

The Basics

Start: Great Barrington, in the state's southwestern corner. Park in the center of town, along the main street or in the parking lot two blocks to the west. Distances are measured from the Chamber of Commerce information booth at the intersection of the town's main street, routes 7 and 41 combined, and Taconic St.
Length: 34.9 or 30.1 miles
Terrain: Rolling hills with only two climbs longer than a half mile. Smooth road surface and light traffic.
Food: Downtown Sheffield, strung along Rte. 7 at 11.5 miles,

offers several options, including a small grocery store and a luncheonette.

Miles & Directions

- 0.0 From the Chamber of Commerce information booth, ride west on Taconic Street, following the signs toward Alford and Simon's Rock. Pass beneath a railway bridge as the road begins to climb, and stay left at the first fork, following the sign toward the local hospital.
- 0.3 Bear right with Taconic St. toward Simon's Rock as the road continues to climb.
- 0.8 Top of hill; begin quick descent. Taconic St. becomes Alford Rd.
- 1.5 Left onto Hurlburt at bottom of initial, steep hill. Be sure you don't go so fast that you miss this turn.
- 3.5 Right on Rte. 71, soon passing a midcornfield airport on the right.
- 5.0 Sharp left onto Creamery Rd.
- 6.7 Bear right onto Rte. 23 into South Egremont for a short distance, looking for the next left turn.
- 6.8 Turn left onto a side road at the point where Rte. 23 curves to the right into the village. This road ends in one block at the Egremont Inn.
- 6.9 Left onto Sheffield–South Egremont Rd. opposite the Egremont Inn. With the exception of one small hill, this is a completely flat road for the next 3.3 miles.
- 10.2 Bear right onto Rte. 7 into Sheffield after crossing railroad tracks.
- 11.4 Left onto County Rd. For a visit to Sheffield's grocery store and luncheonette on the right side of Rte 7, continue straight for a short distance.
- 12.0 Cross concrete bridge over Housatonic River.
- 12.3 Continue straight on County Rd.

To ride the longer option, which adds 4.7 miles and a steeper climb to the ride, bear right here onto Hewins St. for

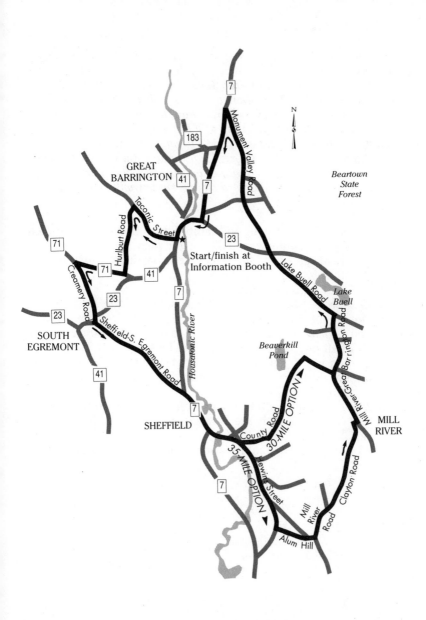

2.9 miles. Bear left onto Alum Hill Rd., which takes you over a short ridge, for 1.2 miles. Turn left onto Mill River Rd. for 0.9 miles. After the tiered barn on your left, turn left up Clayton Rd., which then becomes Mill River Rd., for 2.9 miles. Turn right across bridge into the four corners town of Mill River, then turn left up Mill River–Great Barrington Rd. for 1.5 miles. Then bear right, staying with Mill River–Great Barrington Rd. The shorter ride option joins from the left here, and you can continue with the directions below, although your cumulative distance ridden will be 4.7 miles more.

- 13.0 Continue straight on County Rd. as Home Rd. bears left. County Rd. climbs gradually for the next 3.0 miles.
- 16.8 Bear left onto Mill River–Great Barrington Rd. after the flat stretch by a cow pasture.
- 18.6 Left onto Lake Buell Rd.
- 21.3 Cross Rte. 23 with caution and continue straight onto Monument Valley Rd. Look for views of Monument Mountain's rocky outcroppings to the left in about 1.0 miles.
- 25.7 Left onto Rte. 7 toward Great Barrington at T. Ride with caution to the right on this road's broad shoulder. Be certain to stay to the right especially on the steep descent midway back to town.
- 28.8 Bear right with Rte. 7 as Rte. 23 joins from the left.
- 29.4 Turn left with Rte. 7 as it crosses a bridge over the Housatonic.
- 30.1 Arrive back at information booth at intersection of Rte. 7 and Taconic St.

15

Great Barrington
Josh Billings Cruise

Great Barrington—Alford—West Stockbridge
Glendale—Housatonic—Great Barrington

The Great Barrington Josh Billings Cruise is an adapted version of the Great Josh Billings RunAground, a bike-canoe-run triathalon that attracts nearly two thousand entrants to the southwestern corner of Massachusetts every fall. This cruise follows the RunAground's cycling course almost to Stockbridge. It then turns south onto Route 183, a smooth back road that rolls along the shaded banks of the Housatonic River, to complete a loop back to Great Barrington.

From the official Josh Billings starting line at the intersection of Route 7 and Taconic Street in Great Barrington, the course heads uphill toward the town of Alford and Simon's Rock. Taconic Street climbs for nearly a mile. Imagine struggling up this hill with 600 other cyclists all jockeying for a position at the front following the RunAground's mass start.

Riding at your leisure, you will be able to enjoy some of the sights the racers barely have time to take in. Nineteenth-century summer homes and hillside farms line the back roads from Great Barrington to West Stockbridge. Descending along West Center and Maple Hill roads after 9 miles, the landscape opens up to offer fine views toward Monument Mountain, October Mountain State Forest, and the rest of the Berkshire range.

Crossing over the William River, the course passes through West Stockbridge, humble cousin to Stockbridge, the aristocrat of Berkshire towns. Here, RunAground racers would be gearing down in anticipation of the steep half-mile climb at the far end of this main-street stretch. You should gear down too, but you can stop as well for a rest and snack at the Public Market on the right.

Following the steep climb and long descent along Route 102 east, you could easily detour into Stockbridge by passing the turnoff for Route 183 south. In Stockbridge, take a rest on the broad veranda of the historic Red Lion Inn. Illustrator Norman Rockwell, who moved here from Arlington, Vermont, in 1953, was a cycling enthusiast. Town historians report that he regularly led other bikers along his favorite roads. Stockbridge now sponsors every June a short and leisurely ride recreating his tour through town. Return along Route 102 to get back on course.

To take in some Berkshires culture on the way back to Great Barrington, pay a visit to Chesterwood, in the town of Glendale, 18 miles into the ride. Chesterwood is the 1920s summer estate of Daniel Chester French, sculptor of Washington, D.C.'s Lincoln Memorial and Lexington's Minute Man statue. His home, studio, and sculpture gallery and the surrounding grounds are open daily during the summer season.

The ride's final miles parallel the cool and shaded banks of the Housatonic River. Note the turn-of-the-century railroad and mill buildings dotting the banks of the river below the town of Housatonic. The Rising Paper Company Mill, on the right at 23 miles, is a good example of Victorian factory construction.

The Great Josh Billings RunAground is held every September. For details and information on how to enter, contact the Arcadia Bike Shop in Lenox (413-637-3010).

The Basics

Start: As with the Monument Valley Ramble, park in the center of Great Barrington, along the town's main street or in the public lot on its western end. Distances are measured from the traffic light at the intersection of the town's main street, routes 7 and 41 combined, and Taconic St.

Length: 27.0 miles.

Terrain: Rolling hills, but with only two climbs of more than a half mile in length. The first marks the very beginning of the tour, the second, its middle. Smooth road surface and light traffic. Classic Berkshires countryside.

Food: The Public Market, in West Stockbridge at 14.2 miles, is a good midway snack stop.

Miles & Directions

- 0.0 From Great Barrington's main street, routes 7 and 41 combined, turn west onto Taconic Street, following signs toward Alford and Simon's Rock. Pass beneath a railway bridge as the road begins to climb, and stay left at the first fork, following the sign toward the local hospital.
- 0.3 Bear right with Taconic St. toward Simon's Rock as the road continues to climb.
- 0.8 Top of hill; begin quick descent. Taconic St. becomes Alford Rd.
- 3.9 Bear left onto West Rd. at the fork as you enter the small village of Alford. (East Rd. forks downhill to the right.)
- 4.3 Stay right with West Rd.
- 8.7 Continue straight as dirt road turns left.
- 9.1 Watch out for the patch of dirt road in front of the Alford Brook Club.
- 9.3 Turn left at T onto West Center Rd. Beautiful northerly views up the Berkshire Range for the next several miles.
- 10.8 Bear right onto Maple Hill Rd. as West Center Rd. turns left.
- 12.6 Right onto Rte. 102E at T.
- 13.4 Rte. 102 crosses the Massachusetts Turnpike and descends toward West Stockbridge.
- 13.9 Right at flashing red light, onto combined rtes. 102 and

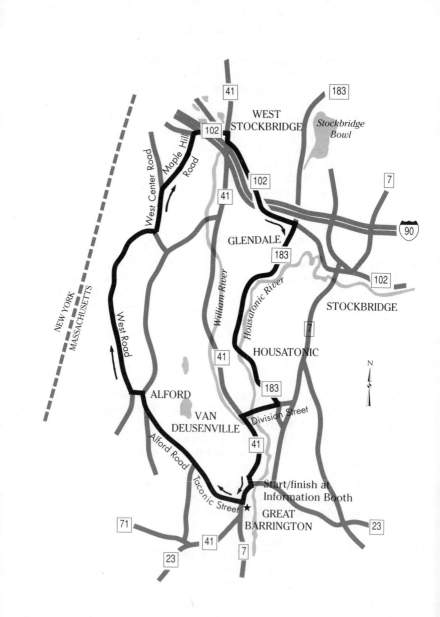

41. Follow this road across the William River and right into West Stockbridge. The Public Market, on the right at 14.2 miles, is a good place to stop for a snack.

- 14.6 Continue straight with Rte. 102E as Rte. 41 turns right toward Great Barrington.

To shave a few miles and one long hill off this route, you may turn right onto Rte. 41 and follow this road all the way back to Great Barrington.

- 15.0 Begin one-half-mile climb. Rte. 102E expands to two lanes here. Stay on the broad smooth shoulder to the right. The climb is rewarded with an even longer downhill.
- 17.3 Turn right onto Rte. 183S at the flashing orange light, following the sign toward Great Barrington and Canaan. (Continue straight on Rte. 102 to detour into Stockbridge.)
- 18.0 Pass through Glendale. Chesterwood, the 1920s summer estate of the sculptor of the Lincoln Memorial, is worth a detour here.
- 19.0 Rte. 183 joins the bank of Housatonic River.
- 21.4 Staying with Rte. 183, turn left at stop sign opposite Pleasant Street Market in the town of Housatonic. Pass beneath railroad bridge, cross the river, and follow the road around to the right on the other side.
- 23.7 Turn right onto Division St. back across the Housatonic River into Van Deusenville.
- 24.7 Turn left onto Rte. 41S toward Great Barrington.
- 26.3 Continue straight as Rte. 7S merges into Rte. 41 from the left for the final mile into Great Barrington.
- 27.0 Ride ends back at intersection of combined routes 7 and 41 with Taconic Ave.

Greylock Mountain Classic

Williamstown—Greylock State Reservation
New Ashford—Williamstown

Far in the state's northwestern corner, 3,500-foot-high Mount Greylock looms over North Adams and Williamstown. It is a rarity among New England mountains in that a road crosses its highest point, making it possible to chart a dramatic circuit ride. Just to the west, the Taconic Trail section of Route 2 crosses the mountains that separate New York from Massachusetts. Taken singly or as back-to-back weekend rides, the Greylock Mountain Classic and the following Taconic Mountain Classic will test your stamina while leading you through the scenic northern reaches of the Berkshire range.

The Mount Greylock State Reservation is a rugged nature preserve that attracts hikers, campers, fly-casters, and even hang gliders. The 37-mile Greylock Mountain Classic ride features its ascent right at the start. The narrow Notch Road winds its way up Greylock's wooded northern flank, climbing 2,800 feet at an average grade of 6 percent in 8 tough miles. As you pedal through the shadows, it can be difficult to believe that these thousands of hillside acres were once mostly cleared by farming and lumbering. Watch out for hikers, as the Appalachian Trail and other wilderness paths cross the road at several points.

From Notch Road, Summit Road leads to the Appalachian Mountain Club lodge on the mountain's windswept summit. The

360-degree views here are too magnificent to pass up out of eagerness to start the descent. Climb the memorial tower, which marks the highest point in Massachusetts, for the ultimate view. The lodge snack bar and the grassy areas around the summit make this an ideal spot to stop for lunch and chat with the congregated hikers and campers and those who have just driven up for the view.

From Greylock's summit, the Greylock Mountain Classic loops downhill virtually all the way back to Williamstown. Rockwell Road zips from the summit to Route 7 in a fast 10 miles. Route 7N carries a fair bit of traffic. It is scenic, though, and offers a broad paved shoulder for an additional 10 gradually downhill miles to the junction with Route 43. Also called Green River Road, this "low road" to Williamstown—Route 7 continuing into town is the high road—offers an ideal warm-down stretch. It follows the stream from which it takes its name for the final 5 miles to Main Street.

The climb up Mount Greylock is extremely difficult—so difficult, in fact, that competitive athletes can't resist the challenge. Notch Road from North Adams to Greylock's summit is now the centerpiece of two annual races. The Mount Greylock Hill Climb bike race is held every September. Runners tackle the mountain in their annual Mount Greylock Road Race, normally held in August.

The Basics

Start: Williamstown, in the state's far northwestern corner, at the intersection of routes 2 and 7. From Boston, follow Rte. 2W through Greenfield and North Adams. From southern New England, follow Rte. 7N through Pittsfield. Park in the public lot at the end of Spring St., the town's main shopping street, located directly opposite the Williams College campus.
Length: 37.2 miles.
Terrain: Features 7-mile climb of Mt. Greylock. Rest of ride is mainly downhill.

Food: Appalachian Mountain Club lodge at peak of Mt. Grey-lock.

Miles & Directions

- 0.0 From public parking at end of Spring St., pedal back up to Rte. 2 and turn right.
- 1.4 Turn right on Luce Rd., just after turn for Adams Rd.
- 2.1 Luce Rd. bears left and turns into countryside.
- 3.7 Pass reservoir on right, a good resting spot before climb.
- 4.2 Bear right at fork as Luce Rd. joins Notch Rd.
- 5.3 Turn right at fork, following sign into Mt. Greylock State Reservation. Climb steepens.
- 7.1 Cross Appalachian Trail. Watch out for hikers!
- 10.6 Cross Overlook Trail and begin to cross ridge.
- 11.4 Left at stop sign to summit and AMC lodge.
- 12.3 Arrive at AMC lodge parking lot.
- 13.3 Turning back downhill after a visit to the summit, stay left at intersection with Notch Rd.
- 20.7 Pass Visitor's Center on left, continuing straight.
- 21.8 Stay left with main road.
- 22.5 Turn right on Rte. 7 toward Williamstown.
- 24.7 Begin gradual descent for next 7.7 miles to turnoff for Rte. 43.
- 32.4 Turn right onto Rte. 43N into Williamstown. This is a more relaxing option than continuing on Rte. 7 for final stretch into Williamstown.
- 37.0 Turn left on Rte. 2.
- 37.1 Turn left on Spring St.
- 37.2 Arrive at public parking.

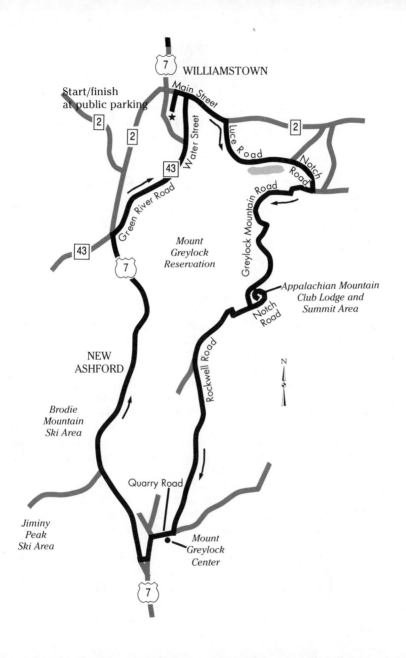

17

Taconic Mountain Classic

Williamstown—Berlin—Petersburg Williamstown

Just to the west of Mount Greylock, the Taconic Trail section of Route 2 appears on most maps as but a squiggle of roadway crossing the New York–Massachusetts border. In fact, though, this 10-mile stretch of road features a thigh-burning climb and blistering descent across a little-known stretch of the Berkshires called the Taconic Range.

Choose either the 45-mile route that crosses the mountains or a shorter 30-mile loop that stays in their shadows. Both start out along Route 43, the shady "low road" from Williamstown. Crossing Route 7, the course follows a broad valley floor, roller-coastering along in a long straight line. If you are out for a training ride, this is a good place to shift onto your big chainring and practice pushing over the rises, then accelerating down the dips in the road.

The solid wall of mountains on your right gives way 14 miles later, soon after you pass the turnoff for Brodie Mountain ski resort (and for this ride's shorter option). Cross into New York with no climb at all, sprinting for the *Welcome to the Empire State* sign.

Route 22 rolls northward along the western flank of the mountains you've just circled. You may begin to wonder whether the mass of forest and rock rising on your right will ever give way again and allow you to close the loop.

The answer will become apparent as you turn right onto the Taconic Trail section of Route 2. In the small town of Petersburg, you may find a small group of children cheering you along as the road begins to wind up the mountainside. Ride slowly and defensively to conserve your strength for the long climb ahead. Soon the only sounds will be those of your deep breaths, your spinning wheels, and the wind blowing through the pines.

Four miles later, the climb ends with a clear and dramatic view across the valley to Mount Greylock on the other side. Pause briefly to take it in before collecting your reward, the long sweeping descent back toward Williamstown.

The Taconic Mountain Classic's shorter option circles the valley between the Taconic Range and Mount Greylock. This moderate ride features several rolling uphills and a long, gradual descent along Route 7 back toward Williamstown. This course links the Taconic Mountain Classic with the Greylock Mountain Classic, as it shares a long leg with each.

The Basics

Start: Williamstown, in the state's far northwestern corner, at the intersection of routes 2 and 7. From Boston, follow Rte. 2W through Greenfield and North Adams. From southern New England, follow Rte. 7N through Pittsfield. Park in the public lot at the end of Spring St., the town's main shopping street, located directly opposite the Williams College campus.

Length: 45.3 miles or 27.8-mile option.

Terrain: An unforgiving 4-mile climb at the end of an otherwise rolling ride makes the longer option a challenging tour for the serious cyclist. The shorter option features several long, gradual climbs but no major obstacles.

Food: Pack a snack, as there are no recommended rest stops on this route.

Miles & Directions

- 0.0 From public parking on Spring St., turn right onto Rte. 2E.
- 0.1 Turn right onto Rte. 43S, Water St.
- 4.6 Cross Rte. 7, continuing south on Rte. 43. Follow Rte. 7 down the side of this valley floor for the next 14 miles.
- 12.9 Pass Brodie Mountain Rd. on the right.

   To complete the shorter and relatively flat 27.8-mile option, turn left here. Follow Brodie Mountain Rd. for 3.4 miles to Rte. 7. Turn left onto Rte. 7N and follow it 6.7 miles back to the intersection with Rte. 43. Then backtrack on Rte. 43 for 4.6 miles to Williamstown. Turn left onto Rte. 2 and left again onto Spring St.

- 18.6 Cross into New York State.
- 19.1 Turn right onto Rte. 22N, toward Berlin and Cherry Plain, at the stoplight. Stay on Rte. 22 as it rolls straight north for the next 16 miles along the opposite flank of the mountains.
- 29.1 Pass through Berlin.
- 35.2 Immediately after passing beneath a stone overpass, turn right on Main St. to join Rte. 2E. A sign for Rte. 2 and Petersburg will alert you to this turn off Rte. 22. Main St. will merge into Rte. 2 in just a short stretch.
- 35.5 Pass through village of Petersburg and begin climb. The ascent takes place in two big steps. The first, short and steep, passes through hillside fields. The second climbs steadily and unforgivingly through a thick forest.
- 38.4 Top of climb. Sign points toward junction with Rte. 7, a 4-mile descent away. Pull over for a view toward Mt. Greylock on the other side of the valley.
- 41.3 Turn left onto combined routes 7 and 2N into Williamstown.
- 43.7 Enter Williamstown at the traffic circle opposite the Williams Inn. Turn right with Rte. 2 just before Rte. 7 turns away toward Vermont.
- 44.1 Turn right onto Spring St.
- 44.2 Return to parking lot at end of Spring St.

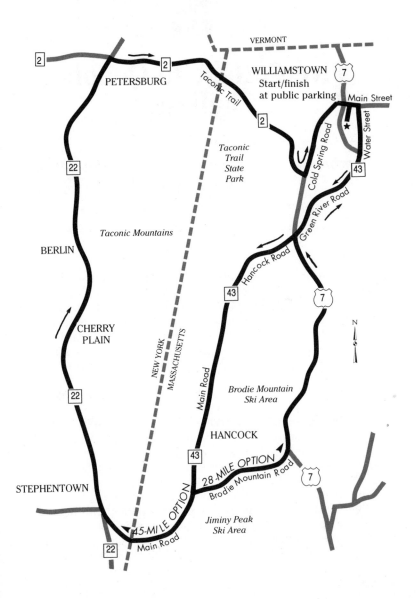

18

Five-College to Quabbin Challenge

Amherst—Belchertown—Bondsville—Ware
Quabbin Reservation
Belchertown—Pelham—Amherst

In the heart of Massachusetts, just east of the Connecticut River, lies the vast Quabbin Reservoir. Engineers created the reservoir in the 1930s by flooding the Swift River and drowning the four towns along its course. Quabbin is now the centerpiece of a large wilderness area, and the more than fifty islands that stud its surface are home to wild turkey and deer. The observation tower on Quabbin Hill rivals the summit of Mount Greylock as vantage point for the most panoramic view in the Commonwealth. Only the bald eagles that regularly soar above Quabbin's waters enjoy a better view.

Quabbin is an Indian word meaning "a lot of water." From the tower, it is clear that this reservoir is aptly named. Its 412 billion gallons of water stretch as far as the eye can see. Quabbin Reservoir Park, which encompasses the reservoir's southern end, includes the observation tower, two huge dams, a new Visitors Center, and miles of hiking trails. All are accessible from the 7-mile-long stretch of road that loops around the park's boundary.

The Five-College to Quabbin Challenge starts and ends at the Amherst town green, a focal point for the region's educational culture. The neighboring towns of Amherst, Northampton, and

South Hadley are home to nearly 35,000 students of Amherst, Hampshire, Mount Holyoke, and Smith colleges and the University of Massachusetts. The Five-College to Quabbin Challenge connects this community with the waterside wilderness of the Quabbin Reservoir Park.

The back roads in between wend their way through farms and woods, alongside rivers stocked with trout, and past small lakes lined with weekend cottages. Although officially a 55-mile tour, you may shorten this to 30 miles by starting in Belchertown and riding just the ride's southern loop. In Belchertown, park along the town green on Route 202. Start out riding south along this road, picking up the directions at 14.5 miles on the full route. Then, heading west on Route 9 after a visit to the reservoir, turn left on Route 202 back into Belchertown rather than right toward Pelham and Amherst. Although 25 miles shorter, this loop includes most of the highlights of the longer ride.

The Basics

Start: Amherst, just east of Northampton, in the state's center. Follow I-91 north from Springfield and the Massachusetts Turnpike (I-90) or south from Greenfield and Rte. 2. From Northampton, take Rte. 9E to Amherst. Park around the Amherst town green, at the intersection of routes 9 and 116, or down one of the nearby side streets.
Length: 55.0 or 30.0 miles.
Terrain: Mildly rolling hills and many long flat stretches. The longest climb is just under a mile long, up Cold Spring Road.
Food: Several choices in Belchertown, at 14.5 miles, and in Bondsville, at 21.9 miles. For a snack to fuel the final miles try the Dairy Queen at 43.5 miles.

Miles & Directions

■ 0.0 From the Amherst town green, ride east on Rte. 9. You should shortly pass beneath a railroad bridge.

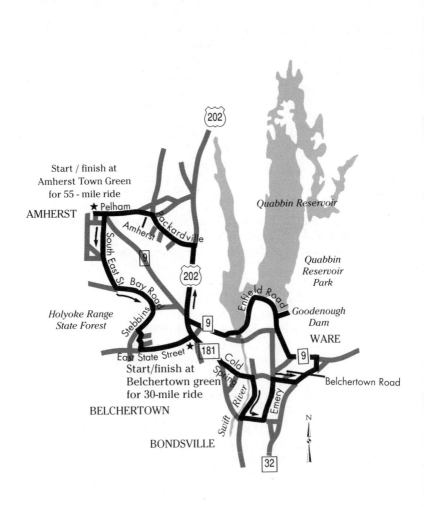

Start / finish at
Amherst Town Green
for 55 - mile ride

AMHERST

★ Pelham

Amherst

Packardville

202

South East St

Bay Road

9

202

Holyoke Range
State Forest

Stebbins

Quabbin Reservoir

Quabbin
Reservoir
Park

Enfield Road

Goodenough
Dam

9

WARE

East State Street ★

181

9

Start/finish at
Belchertown green
for 30-mile ride

Cold

Spring

Belchertown Road

BELCHERTOWN

Swift River

Emery

BONDSVILLE

N

32

- 0.9 Right on South East St. at the first light. Enjoy the views to the left along this nice flat stretch.
- 3.0 Stay left at the fork.
- 3.3 Bear left at Old South Church.
- 5.2 Left onto Bay Rd. as South East St. ends.
- 7.9 Right onto Stebbins Rd., clearly marked at the crest of a short hill.
- 9.7 Left onto "A" Rd. immediately after crossing the town line into Granby.
- 10.0 Stay right at the fork.
- 10.6 Right at the T onto Boardman Rd.
- 11.1 Left onto Rte. 202, here named East State St.
- 13.5 Continue straight as Rte. 21 joins from the right.
- 14.5 Right at the stoplight onto Rte. 181S. toward Palmer and Bondsville. You are now in Belchertown, a nice spot for a snack. There is a Cumberland Farms store just to the left of this intersection. Detour further to the left for a rest on the quarter-mile-long town green.

This ride's shorter 30-mile option starts and ends here, at the Belchertown green. Follow directions below back to Belchertown, riding the lower half of the full tour's figure-eight loop.

- 14.8 Stay on Rte. 181S as it curves to the left for a nice down-hill run. South Main St. forks to the right toward Three Rivers.
- 16.9 Left onto Cold Spring Rd. at the crest of a short hill. This road begins to climb through a hillside orchard.
- 17.7 Stay left at the fork. You should now begin to descend through a thick woods.
- 19.0 Cross single-lane bridge over the Swift River. Approach the bridge slowly, as there are likely to be fishermen along its rails. Turn right on the far side, as another road continues straight and uphill. Follow this unmarked road along the bank of the Swift River and then straight through the small town of Bondsville.
- 21.9 Left at the T as Rte. 181S bears right. There is a large white church directly at this intersection.

- 23.4 Left on Emery St. just after crossing railroad tracks. This left occurs just before the pond on the left.
- 24.6 Pass the tiny Palmer Metropolitan Airport on the right.
- 26.0 Right, downhill, onto Belchertown Rd., which is unmarked at this intersection.
- 26.6 Merge to the right.
- 27.5 Left at end onto Rte. 32N.
- 29.7 Left immediately after passing the McDonald's on the left. This road cuts over to Rte. 9W.
- 29.8 Left onto Rte. 9W toward Belchertown.
- 33.7 Right onto road leading into Quabbin Reservoir Park. This road passes between two stone pillars in among the trees.
- 34.5 Continue straight past the turnoff for Goodenough Dam. Or you may detour for an approximately 4-mile trip to the dam and back. Continuing straight toward the Summit Rd. and Winsor Dam, be sure to stop for the views at the several parking areas along the way.
- 37.1 Ride through the rotary and onto the road toward the Summit Area parking lot. This is a short, steep climb.
- 37.5 Arrive at the summit overlook area. The observation tower here, open to the public, offers 360-degree views of the entire region. From the summit, coast back down to the rotary.
- 37.9 Ride around the rotary and exit onto the road descending toward the Winsor Dam.
- 39.3 Immediately after passing the Winsor Dam spillway, turn right toward and then across the dam.
- 40.4 Right onto Rte. 9.
- 43.5 Right at stoplight onto Rte. 202N toward Athol. There is a Dairy Queen at this intersection.

Turn left here to return to Belchertown if you are riding this ride's shorter 30-mile option.

- 46.9 "Entering Pelham."
- 48.0 Left on Packardville Rd. Although marked, this narrow

turnoff is hard to spot. Look for the small "Packardville Corner" sign on the left. You should pass a small lake in just a half mile.

- 49.0 Stay right at this fork, toward Rte. 116 and Amherst, and stay right again at each of the two merges that follow in the next 2 miles.
- 51.2 Left at T onto Amherst Rd.
- 54.0 Continue straight through intersection with North East St.
- 55.0 Arrive back at town green in the center of Amherst.

19

Lincoln to Great Brook Farm Ramble

Lincoln—Concord—Carlisle—Concord
Lincoln

The Lincoln to Great Brook Farm Ramble is one of several rides recommended by the Lincoln Guide Service bike and nordic ski shop in Lincoln. The shop rents road and mountain bikes, mostly to Bostonians seeking a day's escape from the city. Owner Mike Farney is an accomplished veteran at selecting ideal touring routes. Ask him as well about international tours, of which he has led many.

Lincoln, only a half hour from downtown Boston, is an ideal starting point for rides extending in every direction through a landscape of woods and fields, country cottages and estates. The Lincoln Guide Service makes available maps and directions for a dozen local rides. The Allis Loop, Olympian John Allis's favorite training ride, passes through some of the countryside just south of Lincoln center.

You are likely to meet up with any number of other cyclists along these roads. The Charles River Wheelmen club organizes weekly Sunday morning rides for which Concord is a favorite destination. Once, at Walden Pond, the lawn was taken over by nearly a hundred cyclists. They were resting while "riding for world peace" from Cambridge to Concord and back.

One club conducts a time-trial racing series in Concord on

Tuesday evenings during the summer. This ride's shorter version follows the time-trial course along the Concord–Lowell Road, Route 225, and Monument Street, although in reverse. If you ride any loop regularly, timing yourself on the same 5- or 10-mile stretch every week will help you gauge improvement in fitness over time. Try it on either or both legs of this stretch between Concord and Carlisle.

The Lincoln to Great Brook Farm tour passes through a landscape rich with history. The first stop is Walden Pond, where Henry David Thoreau took his retreat from civilization and wrote *Walden* from 1845 to 1847. Walden Pond is now a popular state park. Its sandy swimming beach draws hundreds on summer weekends. A mile beyond the Concord green on Monument Street, be sure to turn left down a short path to the Old North Bridge Historical Site and the Concord Battleground.

Here, on the morning of April 19, 1775, a group of provincial minutemen met a column of British regulars. The redcoats had been dispatched from Concord to seize a stockpile of armaments and supplies that the provincials had secreted at the Barrett Farm on the other side of the Concord River. A quick exchange of musket shot sent the British running back to town. Thus was "the shot heard round the world" fired, on a wooden bridge across a quiet river outside of Concord. A visitor information center is located up a short road to the left as you cross the Concord River on Monument Street. The Barrett Farm was located at the near right corner of the intersection of Strawberry Hill and Barrett's Mill roads at the 22-mile point on the longer option of this ride.

Today the countryside here is quiet, if not exactly undiscovered. Even after you've ridden this route many times, there is always a new sight along the way—the Concord River flooding its banks after heavy rains, people planting crops on the river's plain as seen from high on Monument Street, newborn colts rolling in a pasture, Canada geese swooping through the trees to land with a splash on a pond.

You may see these sights and more on either route, the

shorter time-trial loop or the longer, back-roads ride that meanders past Great Brook Farm.

The Basics

Start: Lincoln, on the western edge of Boston's Rte. 128. If arriving from Rte. 128, take exit 29 onto Rte. 2W toward Concord. Turn left on Rte. 126, continuing past Walden Pond State Reservation for about 2 miles. Turn left onto Codman St. and left again onto Lincoln Rd. at the first intersection. Park in the public lot on the left immediately after crossing the railroad tracks. Start from the Lincoln Guide Service directly across the street.
Length: 30.2 miles, with a 20.5-mile option that does not extend as far as Great Brook Farm.
Terrain: Rolling hills with no climbs longer than a half mile.
Food: Several choices in Concord at 4.5 or again at 24 miles. If you are riding the longer route, Great Brook Farm sells snacks during the summer season. On the shorter loop, Kendall's Ice Cream stand on Rte. 225 makes for an excellent midway stop; it is on the right at 10 miles.

Miles & Directions

- 0.0 From Lincoln Guide Service ride west, crossing the railroad tracks, on Lincoln Road. If you arrived in Lincoln by the directions given above, you'll start this ride by retracing the route to Walden Pond.
- 0.2 Right onto Codman Rd., passing the historic Codman House on the right.
- 0.9 Right onto Rte. 126.
- 2.7 Walden Pond, with lakeside beach and facilities, on the left. Continue on Rte. 126 across Rte. 2 at traffic light.
- 3.5 At bottom of steep hill, continue straight toward Concord as main road forks left.

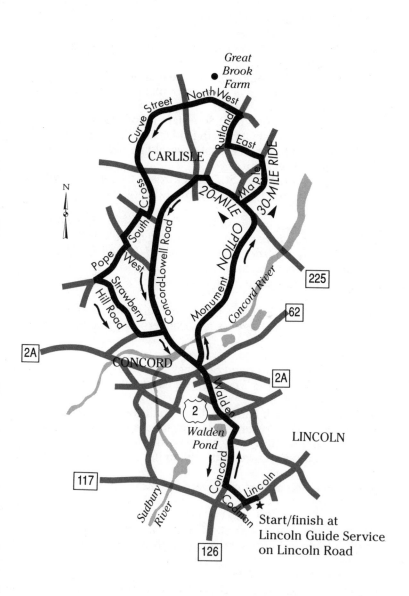

Great
Brook
Farm

Curve Street   North West

Rutland

East

CARLISLE

Maple

30-MILE RIDE

N

Cross

20-MILE OPTION

South

Concord-Lowell Road

Pope

West

225

Strawberry

Monument

Concord River

Hill Road

62

2A

CONCORD

Walden

2A

2

Walden
Pond

LINCOLN

117

Concord

Sudbury
River

Lincoln

Codman

126

★ Start/finish at
Lincoln Guide Service
on Lincoln Road

- 4.1 Right onto Heywood St. after passing Concord fire station on the right.
- 4.3 Left onto Lexington St. at T, just after passing town information booth. There is a water fountain by the monument on the town green on the left.
- 4.6 Right onto Monument St. at far end of green. Continue on Monument St. past Old North Bridge and Battleground, across the Concord River, and past several fine old horse farms.
- 9.0 Left on Rte. 225.
- 9.2 Right onto Maple St., a back road, to continue with the longer, back-road route past Great Brook Farm.

If you are riding the shorter, more direct route back to Concord, continue straight on Rte. 225 to the small rotary in Carlisle, then turn onto the Concord–Lowell Rd. back to Concord. From Concord, backtrack to Lincoln following the directions starting at 24.3 miles below.

- 10.5 Right onto Treble Cove Rd. This intersection may be unmarked, but there is a "Dangerous Intersection" sign ahead.
- 10.6 Left onto East St., a more traveled road.
- 11.5 Right onto Rutland St., back onto the back roads.
- 12.5 Left on North West Rd., unmarked but at the first four-way intersection.
- 13.7 Great Brook Farm on the right. Stop for a tour through this working dairy farm or simply for a rest on the grassy lawn by the pond. After visit, continue on North West Rd.
- 14.1 Right onto Lowell Rd. and an immediate left onto Curve St.
- 15.6 Bear left at the fork toward Rte. 225. A big red barn marks this turn.
- 16.4 Left onto Rte. 225 for a short distance.
- 16.7 Right onto Cross St., labeled on a stone marker.
- 17.8 Right at stop sign onto South St., which is unmarked here.
- 18.8 Left onto West St.

- 18.9 Right onto Pope Rd.
- 20.1 Left onto Strawberry Hill Rd. You should pass a yellow farm house on the right following this turn.
- 22.1 Left onto Barrett's Mill Rd., marked by the Minutemen Monument at the intersection.
- 22.8 Right onto Lowell Rd. back through Concord, continuing straight through the intersection on the far side of the town green with the water fountain on your left.
- 24.3 Right onto Heywood St., marked by the Concord information booth on the left just after the turn.
- 24.4 Left onto Walden St. Continue past fire station, straight up hill, across Rte. 2 and onto Rte. 126 past Walden Pond.
- 27.3 Left onto Codman Rd. toward Lincoln.
- 30.0 Left onto Lincoln Rd. and across railroad tracks.
- 30.2 Welcome back to the Lincoln Guide Service.

20

The Allis Loop

Belmont—Waltham—Lincoln—Sudbury
Weston—Waltham—Belmont

Boston's most famous training circuit for racing cyclists is known simply as the Allis Loop. This is the regular workout ride of John Allis, a three-time Olympian and respected dean of the local cycling scene. He rode the course twice daily to prepare for the 1968, 1972, and 1976 Olympic road races. Today it is a favorite training route of the Boston Road Club's women's squad and the Harvard University cycling team, both of which John helps coach.

John first mapped the tour in 1972 by sitting down with a map and tracing what appeared to be the least-trafficked roads leading west from Cambridge. The Loop was originally 40 miles long, the distance he could ride in the two hours he had available before and after work. But with his move to Belmont it became shortened to the current 32 miles.

The Allis Loop is ridden in an infinite number of variations by dozens of local cyclists. The course starts at Belmont Wheel Works, the bike shop John now owns. Alternate starting points include Cambridge, where John has opened a new Wheel Works store, and the green in Weston. From either end, the ride turns west to explore the near-rural suburbs of Lincoln, Sudbury, and Weston. These three towns are the center of the "green belt" west of Boston that offers excellent cycling surprisingly near a major urban center. The Lincoln to Great

Brook Farm Ramble loops through the region's northern townships.

Not just a training circuit, the Allis Loop is conducive to strictly leisurely biking as well. Turn up the driveway of the DeCordova Museum in Lincoln, on Sandy Pond Road, for a quick tour of its sculpture gardens overlooking Sandy Pond. On a clear day, New Hampshire's Mount Monadnock is visible on the horizon from here. Turning left onto Baker Bridge Road, stop at the Gropius House, an early example of modern Bauhaus architecture. Stop on the wood plank bridge across the Sudbury River for the view to either side, where much of the shoreline is protected by the Great Meadows Wildlife Refuge. In Weston, following the rough stretch along Glezen Lane, stop for a rest on the expansive green or at the nearby Friendly's restaurant. Both are favorite meeting places for Sunday morning rides organized by the Charles River Wheelmen.

The Allis Loop offers a pleasant ride no matter what pace you keep or how often you ride, whether twice a day or once a week.

The Basics

Start: Belmont Wheel Works bike shop in Belmont, at 480 Trapelo Rd., just east of Trapelo's intersection with Pleasant St. Belmont is located between routes 2 and 20, on the inside of Boston's beltway, Rte. 128.
Length: 33.2 miles.
Terrain: Rolling suburban and rural roads west of Boston.
Food: A pizza place and convenience store are on the right at the intersection of Rte. 117 and Sudbury Rd. at 14.0 miles, and a Friendly's restaurant is on the right in Weston at 24.8 miles.

Miles & Directions

- 0.0 From the Belmont Wheel Works, ride west on Trapelo Rd.
- 0.2 Turn sharp right, uphill, onto Pleasant St.

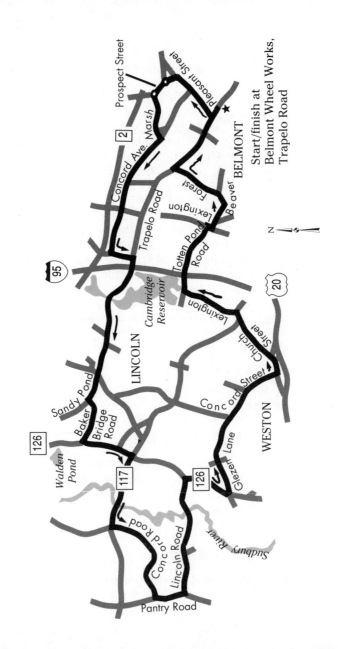

Start/finish at Belmont Wheel Works, Trapelo Road

- 1.3 Turn left onto Clifton St. at the stoplight, opposite Leonard St.
- 1.6 Bear left through the rotary, continuing uphill on Prospect St.
- 2.0 Bear left onto Marsh St., next to the Belmont Hill School, at the second rotary.
- 3.1 Turn right at the T onto Concord Ave., just after crossing Winter St. Continue on Concord Avenue for almost 3 miles, crossing Waltham St. and then passing within sight of Rte. 2 on the right.
- 6.0 Turn left onto Spring St. as Concord Ave. ends.
- 6.5 Turn right onto Trapelo Rd. Follow Trapelo for almost 3 miles, crossing the Cambridge Reservoir, to its end in Lincoln center.
- 9.3 Trapelo ends at intersection with Lincoln Rd. Cross this intersection onto Sandy Pond Rd. toward the DeCordova Museum.
- 10.0 Turn left onto Baker Bridge Rd., which is unmarked at this end. This is the first possible left turn after you pass the entrance to the DeCordova Museum on the right.
- 11.1 Left onto Rte. 126 at T. A right turn here would lead you to Walden Pond and Concord. Ride past the left turn for Codman Rd.
- 12.3 Turn right onto Rte. 117 at the stoplight.
- 14.0 At the next stoplight, turn left onto Concord Rd. Sudbury Rd. turns right. This is Concord Crossing. The pizza place and convenience store on the right are good for snacks.
- 16.3 Bear left with Concord Rd. at the T as Pantry Rd. turns right.
- 17.1 Turn left onto Lincoln Rd. at Lincoln-Sudbury Regional High School.
- 19.2 Cross the wood plank bridge over the Sudbury River, pausing for the view, as Lincoln Rd. becomes Sherman Bridge Rd.
- 19.9 Turn right onto Rte. 126, keeping a sharp eye out for the next left turn.

- 22.0 Turn left onto Glezen Lane, a rough and winding road. This becomes Sudbury Rd.
- 23.0 When you see the classical facade of the Campion Center, a former monastery, continue straight past it. You will have merged into Concord St., which then curves downhill to the right.
- 23.8 Bear right, staying on Concord St.
- 24.6 Turn left at the T, riding into the center of Weston.
- 24.9 Turn left onto Church St., which borders the far side of the town green. Follow Church St. as it winds downhill toward Rte. 117.
- 26.1 Right on Rte. 117, named North Ave. here, after crossing the commuter rail tracks at the Kendal Green Station.
- 26.3 Take first possible left, onto Lexington St. This becomes West St. Continue to the T opposite the Cambridge Reservoir.
- 27.7 Jog right onto Winter St. at the reservoir. Winter St. becomes Totten Pond Rd. after crossing the overpass over Rte. 128.
- 29.3 Turn right at the stoplight onto Lexington St., then bear left immediately with Lexington St. as Bacon St. continues straight.
- 29.5 Turn left on Beaver St. toward the Chapel High School.
- 30.3 Bear left onto Forest St. at Bentley College.
- 31.5 Turn right onto Trapelo.
- 33.0 Pass turnoff for Pleasant St. on left and continue on Trapelo back to Belmont.
- 33.2 Arrive at Belmont Wheel Works on the left.

21

Cape Ann Cruise

Manchester—Magnolia—Gloucester
East Gloucester—Rockport
Annisquam—Gloucester—Manchester

The Fisherman's Memorial on Gloucester's Pavilion Beach speaks for all of Cape Ann. Its rough-hewn mariner stands at his ship's wheel, gazing into a storm. He memorializes the more than ten thousand lives this fishing port has lost at sea in its 350-year history. But he also symbolizes the rich heritage of the entire cape, where livelihoods are still extracted from the surrounding ocean.

The Cape Ann Cruise explores the best of Boston's North Shore. This 33-mile or 20-mile loop circles the rocky shores of Cape Ann, where fishermen's cottages and grand summer homes now share the ocean views. The route passes through the working waterfront of Gloucester and the harbor towns of East Gloucester, Rockport, and Annisquam, favorites of artists and tourists alike.

This is the signature ride of the North Shore Cyclists. This club's calendar also includes Sunday morning tours around Beverly, Ipswich, Plum Island, Newburyport, Topsfield, and other north-of-Boston communities. The Charles River Wheelmen pedal past Cape Ann at least once every year. Their early season "Beer and Steamers" ride circles from Reading, into New Hampshire, and back down the North Shore coast.

The 33-mile loop starts in Manchester, not far from one of the area's best beaches. After your ride, pay a visit to Singing Beach, so named for the sound its sand makes as the waves roll ashore. To get there, follow Beach Street for a half mile away from the town center to its end. Walk, as parking is extremely limited. The shorter option starts at the Fisherman's Memorial statue on Gloucester's Pavilion Beach.

From Gloucester, both rides follow the same route around the cape. The opening miles to Rockport pass through East Glouces-ter, on a protected harbor, to the open ocean along Atlantic Road. Here, on rough days, the pounding waves send salt spray up to the road. When it is calmer, you may want to stop for a rest on one of the many grassy spots above the rocks.

Rockport, midway on either ride, enjoys a varied and colorful history. This small town might have become a major east coast city, had a group of promoters a hundred years ago succeeded in their drive to make its harbor home to the U. S. North Atlantic Fleet. A crumbling breakwater off the shore is all that remains of their effort. If you spot a sea monster, you will not have been the first to do so. Twice in the nineteenth century dozens of sober townspeople testified that they had spotted a hundred-foot-long serpent in the local waters. You can learn more about the town's past at the Sandy Bay Historical Museum on King Street.

Halfway between Rockport and Annisquam, turn right off Route 127 for a detour to the rocky headland of Halibut Point. This 54-acre state park is the site of a former granite quarry. Abandoned in 1929, its huge pit is now filled with water. Path-ways lead to a series of expansive granite shelves stepping down into the sea. This is a popular spot for walking, sunning, and picnicking.

The small, charming village of Annisquam is the last stop on the cape. Visit the Lobster Cove Market and Marina overlooking the Annisquam River. The Annisquam connects Ipswich Bay, on the cape's north side, to Gloucester Harbor, to the south. On a sunny day there is a constant parade of boats large and small through this waterway.

Although you'll encounter many other cyclists along this route, bicycling must share with scuba diving the distinction of being Cape Ann's most popular recreational activity. On weekends, wetsuited divers splash around and crawl in and out of almost every protected cove around the cape.

The Cape Ann Cruise is particularly recommended for the spring and the fall, when weekend traffic for the most part subsides. In the summer, try to get an early morning start, as the cape's cool ocean breezes, picturesque towns, and plentiful beaches bring out the crowds.

The Basics

Start: Manchester, off Rte. 128 near its northern end. Park in the commuter rail parking lot on Beach St., just off Rte. 127, downtown. If this lot is full, try the high school parking lot less than a mile east on Rte. 127 on the left. Or park in Gloucester to ride the 20-mile loop.
Length: 33.0 or 20.0 miles.
Terrain: Flat to slightly rolling coastal route. Sections of rough or narrow roadway with heavy summer weekend traffic.
Food: The Lobster Cove Market and Marina, in Annisquam at 22.3 miles, offers sandwiches from its market deli as well as a menu of fried clams, hamburgers, and the like from a casual restaurant with picnic tables facing the waterfront.

Miles & Directions

- 0.0 From the commuter rail parking lot in downtown Manchester, turn right onto Beach Street, crossing the railroad tracks; then turn right onto Rte. 127 toward Gloucester and Rockport.
- 1.4 Right onto Ocean St., a short seaside detour off Rte. 127.
- 2.1 Right back onto Rte. 127 toward Gloucester.
- 2.4 Right on Raymond St. toward Magnolia and the Hammond Castle.

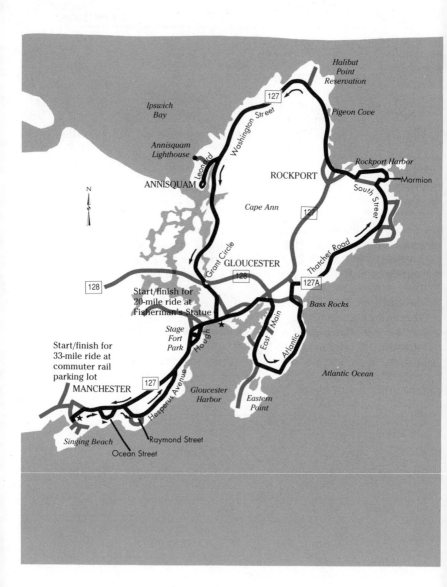

- 2.9 Straight through intersection. (Shore Drive, the sharp right turn, loops bumpily around a point of land that you might want to detour to explore.) Raymond St. becomes Norman Ave.
- 3.4 Bear left onto Hesperus Ave., toward Hammond Castle, on the left in just under a mile.
- 4.8 Right onto Rte. 127.
- 6.5 Entering Gloucester on Rte. 127, pass the town's long Pavilion Beach and its Fisherman's Memorial statue. Stay on Rte. 127 as it turns left and then dips down to Gloucester's Inner Harbor and busy working waterfront. Ride carefully, as this is the most trafficked section of this tour.

The ride's shorter, 20-mile option starts here.

- 7.5 Bear right at light onto East Main St. toward East Gloucester.
- 7.7 Bear right with East Main St. at East Gloucester Square.
- 8.8 Pass turnoff for Rocky Neck on the right.
- 9.1 Turn left onto Farrington Ave. just after passing Niles Beach on the right. You may choose to detour to the right, between the stone pillars, onto Eastern Point Blvd. This 1.3-mile road leads to the lighthouse marking the entrance to Gloucester Harbor.
- 9.5 Turn left onto Atlantic Rd., which passes along a dramatic, rocky coastline for the next couple of miles.
- 11.2 Turn left with Atlantic Rd. as it turns away from the water.
- 11.5 Cross Bass Ave. and continue straight onto Thatcher Rd., Rte. 127A.
- 15.0 Right onto Marmion Way shortly before entering Rockport center.
- 16.0 Right back onto Rte. 127A, now called South St.
- 16.5 Continue straight through downtown Rockport.
- 16.8 Bear right at the fork onto Beach St., staying next to the waterfront, toward Pigeon Cove. A park and bandstand on the left, opposite Rockport's Back Beach, provide a nice spot to stop for a rest.

- 17.1 Right at the stop sign onto Rte. 127 toward Pigeon Cove and Annisquam.
- 21.6 Right at Annisquam Village Church into Annisquam. Although unmarked, this is Leonard St.
- 21.9 Bear left at fork.
- 22.1 Left on Bridgewater St., down a short hill, and right at the bottom, opposite the long wooden footbridge crossing Lobster Cove. The Lobster Cove Market and Marina follows on the left. This enterprise includes both a grocery store with a deli and a casual restaurant, so it is an ideal lunch stop.
- 22.4 Turn right onto Leonard St. at end, bear right at fork, and backtrack to the Annisquam Village Church on Rte. 127. Or you may backtrack from the Lobster Cove Marina, turn right across Lobster Cove on the wooden footbridge, and turn right onto Rte. 127 farther south.
- 23.0 Right onto Rte. 127, here called Washington St., at the Village Church.
- 26.0 Ride halfway around Grant Circle, mindful of the traffic entering and exiting this rotary, and continue onto Rte. 127, Washington St., into the city of Gloucester.
- 26.5 Right onto Centennial Ave.
- 27.0 Right onto Rte. 127, now Western Ave., facing Western Harbor. Cross the short drawbridge spanning the canal that effectively makes Cape Ann an island.

The ride's shorter, 20-mile option ends here.

- 27.3 Left onto Hough Ave., which cuts through the Stage Fort Park waterfront.
- 27.7 Left on Rte. 127 back toward Manchester.
- 33.0 Return to commuter rail parking lot in downtown Manchester.

22

Cape in a Day
(or Two) Classic

Boston—Bourne—Provincetown—Boston

Bostonians will do anything to get to Cape Cod's sandy shores. That includes setting out on a marathon bike ride at the barely gray light of dawn. Dozens do it every year, and not just to avoid the highway traffic they would face driving to the beach. No, they do it because cycling from Boston to the Cape's tip at Provincetown is a challenge too seductive to pass up. This round trip route's first leg is by land and its second by sea; riders return to Boston via ferry. Most participants actually break the ride in two with a youth hostel stay along the way.

This ride has such natural appeal that the Commonwealth of Massachusetts has designated the official Boston–Cape Cod Bikeway. And the greater Boston Council of the American Youth Hostels organizes an annual "Cape in a Day" tour following a somewhat different course. Whether you follow the Boston–Cape Cod Bikeway or join the next Cape in a Day expedition, cycling to Provincetown is an accomplishment you will be able to boast about for a long time to come.

Those who complete the ride remember the groggy early morning passage through Boston's southern suburbs; a pit stop for pastries and juice in Plymouth; that first sight of the Saga-more Bridge arcing above the treetops; the sun beating down during the midday stretch through Sandwich, Barnstable, and Yarmouth; and, finally, the turning up the Cape's hook for the ride's final leg. Some stick to their designated route; others explore or detour onto the Cape Cod Rail Trail, a former railroad track converted to recreation path.

The Youth Hostel group, normally numbering about fifty cyclists, actually saves the ride's final 10 miles for the next day. They retire for the night to the Truro Hostel and enjoy the next morning on the National Seashore, where miles of perfect beach, waves, and grass-covered dunes provide a respite from the previous day's many hours on the road. Following an afternoon pedal to Provincetown, they catch the ferry back to Boston and there say goodbye to the friends made along the way.

Long rides such as this are always best enjoyed in the company of other cyclists. Sign up for the Youth Hostel tour or organize your own group to ride the Boston–Cape Cod Bikeway. The Commonwealth of Massachusetts has published an excellent, detailed, and free map for the entire Bikeway. In addition, the Bikeway's initial stretch to Bourne is marked with signs (look for the green ovals with a bike in the center), and the second segment to Provincetown is marked with arrows painted on the road (look for the arrows with the letter "C" on either side). Addresses for obtaining more information about the Youth Hostel ride or the Bikeway route are given below. Neither route, whether ridden in one day or two, is intended for inexperienced cyclists.

The Basics

Start: The Boston–Cape Cod Bikeway starts at Boston University on Commonwealth Avenue. The Greater Boston Youth Hostel tour takes off from Coolidge Corner in Brookline, at the intersection of Harvard and Beacon streets. Both locations are on the Boston subway's Green Line route.

Length: The Boston–Cape Cod Bikeway measures 135 miles from Boston University to Provincetown. The Youth Hostel tour follows a 122-mile route.

Terrain: Rolling or flat, with no major hills. Both the Boston–

Cape Cod Bikeway and the Youth Hostel route follow low-volume roads once beyond Boston's more congested streets. **Food:** Because this is not a backwoods tour, the choices are too numerous to mention. The Youth Hostel tour traditionally stops at Leo's Bakery in Plymouth, at the Friendly's restaurant by the Sagamore Bridge rotary, and at the Emack & Bolio's ice cream shop in Orleans.

Miles & Directions

Neither a detailed map nor directions are included for this ride.

To obtain a copy of the state's official Boston–Cape Cod Bikeway map, send a business-size, stamped (65 cents), and self-addressed envelope to Cape Cod Map, Department of Transportation Library, 10 Park Plaza, Boston, MA 02116, or simply drop by and pick up a copy.

For information on how to join the annual Youth Hostel ride, write to Touring Director, Greater Boston Council, American Youth Hostels, 1020 Commonwealth Ave., Boston, MA 02215.

23

Tour de Vineyard

A springtime dawn breaks quietly over Martha's Vineyard. Mist rises from the lush fields, revealing deer that have come out to graze. Weathered shingle homes blend into the muted landscape. Rabbits disappear into the scrub oak woods at the approaching sound of your tires humming down the road.

Martha's Vineyard remains a timeless paradise for beachgoers and cyclists alike. Its roads wend their way through woodland and farms, past miles of white sand beaches, around millponds, inlets, and creeks. This triangular island has served as an offshore vacation retreat since the summer religious camp meetings of the last century first introduced the Vineyard to large-scale tourism.

Today, the Vineyard's population grows tenfold, from 7,000 to 70,000 residents, every summer. Although cycling here can be enjoyable at any time of year, the roads are quietest and the weather nicest in the spring and fall.

The Tour de Vineyard offers at least two days of cycling. The first day's ride follows the Up Island Cruise route, exploring the rolling roads of the island's less populated western half. A 25-mile option extends from the ferry landing in Vineyard Haven as far as the fishing village of Menemsha and the summer community of Chilmark. A 39-mile alternative follows the Vineyard's scenic roads as far as Gay Head, where sunset-hued cliffs drop down to the sea. This hilly point of land features some of the island's most dramatic scenery.

The second day's ride is the 28-mile East Island Ramble. This tour follows virtually flat roads around the island's eastern half, exploring the historic and still busy beach communities of Edgartown and Oak Bluffs. The ride follows well-maintained bike paths through the island's state forest and along the oceanfront stretch from Edgartown to Oak Bluffs. An optional 3-mile detour crosses Edgartown Harbor by way of the "On-Time" ferry to visit Chappaquiddick Island.

Each ride represents a daylong excursion, including beach and lunch stops along the way. The easiest way to get to the island is to leave your car in Woods Hole, on the mainland side, and take only your bike across. You are likely to find yourself in the company of other cyclists for the trip. Youth hostel and student cycling groups are regular ferry passengers.

If you would like to start riding on reaching Cape Cod rather than waiting to arrive on Martha's Vineyard, consider following the Boston–Cape Cod Bikeway extension from the Sagamore Bridge to the Woods Hole ferry. (The Cape in a Day [or Two] Classic follows the full length of the Bikeway from Boston to Provincetown, at the Cape's tip.) Start at the youth hostel in Cedarville, just on the mainland side of the Sagamore Bridge. To reach the hostel, turn right off Route 3S onto Clark Road toward Myles Standish State Park. Then turn left onto Long Pond Road, away from the park, and follow it for 6 miles to Carter Bridge Road. Turn right on Carter Bridge and then right again onto Upland Road to the hostel.

Biking from the hostel, turn left on Carter Bridge Road and left again onto Long Pond Road. Then turn right onto the Bikeway, following Hedges Pond Road and Route 3A to the Sagamore Bridge. Walk your bike on the sidewalk across the bridge, turn left on the other side on Adams Road, which leads down to the railroad tracks along the canal, and turn left onto the Canal Service Road toward Woods Hole. From here, follow the Bikeway signs south along the Canal Service Road and Route 28A to the island ferry.

The Woods Hole Steamship Authority runs daily ferries between Woods Hole and Vineyard Haven. The trips lasts forty-five minutes. Some ferries continue on to Oak Bluffs and Nantucket. Passengers traveling by bicycle or on foot do not need reservations. Call the Steamship Authority at 508-405-2022 for information on fares and schedules.

Tour de Vineyard: Up Island Cruise

August 1994

Vineyard Haven—North Tisbury
Menemsha—Lobsterville
Gay Head—West Tisbury—Vineyard Haven

The Basics

Start: The ferry terminal in Vineyard Haven. The several-times-a-day ferry from Woods Hole, at Cape Cod's southwestern tip, is the island's primary link with the mainland. Follow Rte. 28S from Buzzard's Bay to Woods Hole.

Length: 24.7 or 39.3 miles.

Terrain: Gently rolling, generally well-paved roads. No severe climbs.

Food: Stop in Gay Head, this tour's midway point and primary destination, at 21 miles. There are concession stands, a crab shack, and a restaurant here, as well as a picnic area and facilities. Also, Alley's General Store in West Tisbury at 32.9 offers snacks, drinks, and a stoop to sit on.

Miles & Directions

- 0.0 Coming off the Wood's Hole ferry, turn left onto Water St.
- 0.1 Right, following the sign toward West Tisbury, Chilmark, and Gay Head.
- 0.2 Stay left at the fork, merging into South Main St., which soon becomes State Rd.
- 1.4 Scenic turnoff on the right.

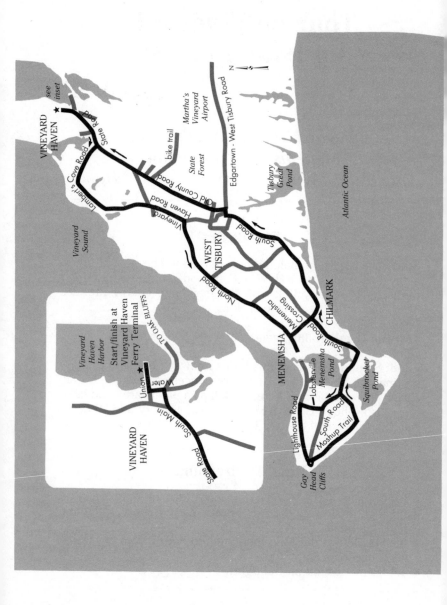

- 1.6 Right on Lambert's Cove Rd.
- 5.9 Right at T onto Vineyard Haven Rd.
- 7.1 Fork right onto North Rd. toward Menemsha. Look for the ancient oak tree in the clearing on your right just before this turn.
- 12.4 Left on Menemsha Crossing Rd. toward Chilmark and Gay Head.

You may detour into the small fishing village of Menemsha simply by continuing straight, downhill, for just under a mile. Double back to this intersection to continue with the tour.

- 13.3 At Beetlebung Corner, turn right on South Rd.

If riding the shorter 24.7-mile option, continue straight onto South Rd. toward West Tisbury, picking up the directions starting at 27.9 miles below.

- 16.4 Sprint for the "Entering Gay Head" sign. Don't miss the views of Menemsha Pond on your right.
- 16.8 Stay right on South Rd. as the Moshup Trail Rd. turns left.
- 18.0 Right on Lobsterville Rd. toward Lobsterville Town Beach for a nice downhill run.
- 18.8 Left, gradually uphill, onto Lighthouse Rd.

For a beachside detour, follow Lobsterville Rd. around to the right as it traces the edge of the Menemsha Bight. This road follows the line of the beach for 2 miles to the narrow channel connecting Menemsha Pond to the Vineyard Sound. Continue the tour by retracing your route and then turning right onto Lighthouse Rd.

- 20.8 Right onto the short loop of road at Gay Head. Look for the lighthouse on your right. Leaving the road, walk your bikes among the concession stands and up the short walk to the Gay Head Cliffs viewing area.

- 21.2 Right at the end of the loop onto the Moshup Trail road, which swoops downhill toward the open ocean. This road offers terrific views of the surf along Gay Head Town Beach for most of the next 2 miles.
- 24.4 Right back onto South Road.
- 27.9 Returning to Beetlebung Corner, turn right with South Road toward West Tisbury.
- 32.9 Arriving in West Tisbury, you may want to stop for a snack and a sit on the front stoop of Alley's General Store on your left.
- 33.0 Continuing through West Tisbury, bear right onto Edgartown Rd. toward Katama and Edgartown.
- 33.3 Left onto Old County Rd., soon after passing the Old Millpond on the left.
- 36.4 Merge right into State Rd., returning to Vineyard Haven.
- 39.2 Turn left onto Water St., opposite the Cumberland Farms store on your right.
- 39.3 Arrive back at ferry terminal.

Tour de Vineyard:
East Island Ramble

Vineyard Haven—North Tisbury
Edgartown—Chappaquiddick
Edgartown—Oak Bluffs—Vineyard Haven

The Basics

Start: The ferry terminal in Vineyard Haven, the same starting point as for the Tour De Vineyard's Up Island Cruise.
Length: 25.3 miles, or 28.3 with Chappaquiddick excursion.
Terrain: Flat coastal and woodland roads. Includes two long sections of well-maintained bike trail.
Food: Nearly endless selection of quick lunch stops at the Edgartown harborfront at 15.0 miles and in Oak Bluffs at 21.5 miles.

Miles & Directions

- 0.0 Coming off the Wood's Hole ferry, turn left onto Water St.
- 0.1 Right, following the sign toward West Tisbury, Chilmark, and Gay Head.
- 0.2 Stay left at the fork, merging into South Main St., which soon becomes State Rd.
- 1.4 Scenic turnoff on the right.
- 1.6 Continue straight onto County Rd. as Lambert's Cove Rd. turns right.
- 2.9 Continue straight onto Old County Rd. as Vineyard Haven Rd. turns right toward Menemsha.

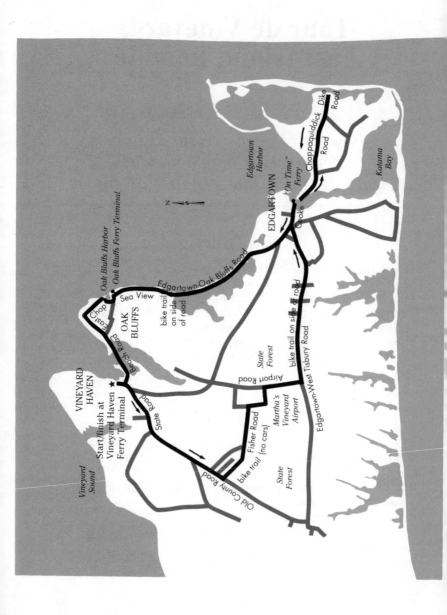

- 3.8 Left onto the Hopps Farm Rd. bike trail through Martha's Vineyard State Forest. As you enter the forest, go straight rather than turning right onto the trail that parallels Old County Rd.
- 6.3 Right, toward Martha's Vineyard Airport, as the trail comes to a T.
- 7.2 Left with the trail as it skirts the airport.
- 8.1 Right onto Airport Rd. or onto the trail paralleling it across the street.
- 10.1 Left onto West Tisbury Rd. or the adjacent bike trail.
- 14.3 Right on Cooke St., following the sign toward Edgartown Center and Chappaquiddick. From here, follow the bicycle route signs through Edgartown's narrow one-way streets to the "On Time" ferry terminal.
- 15.0 Arrive at ferry terminal. After visiting Chappaquiddick Island or simply checking out Edgartown's waterfront, leave the harbor area by following Winter St. and Pease St. to the flagpole at the intersection of Pease and Main sts.

For the 5-mile round trip excursion to Chappaquiddick Island, hop the ferry for the short trip across Edgartown Harbor. Follow the island's only paved road, Chappaquiddick Rd., past the beach club and up a small rise. In 2 miles the road turns sharp right. Continue straight onto Dike Rd., which is unpaved but smooth. It will lead you past a Japanese garden on the left to the infamous Dike Bridge. Lock your bikes for a walk onto expansive East Beach.

- 15.7 Right onto Main St. toward Vineyard Haven and Oak Bluffs.
- 16.3 Fork right onto Edgartown–Oak Bluffs Rd. toward Oak Bluffs. Hop onto the broad, smooth bike trail on the left just a short distance down the road.
- 21.3 Left onto Bluffs Ave. immediately opposite the Oak Bluffs ferry terminal. Then continue straight onto Lake Ave., skirting Oak Bluffs Harbor.
- 21.7 Right onto East Chop Drive, also called Commercial Ave.,

continuing around the harbor. Follow East Chop Drive, which turns into Highland Drive, around the waterfront.

- 22.7 East Chop lighthouse on the right.
- 23.4 Right on Temahigan Ave., toward Vineyard Haven, immediately after Highland Drive turns sharply inland.
- 23.7 Right on Beach Rd. across the long causeway back to Vineyard Haven.
- 25.1 Right on Water St.
- 25.3 Right on Union St. at the Vineyard Haven ferry terminal.

New Hampshire

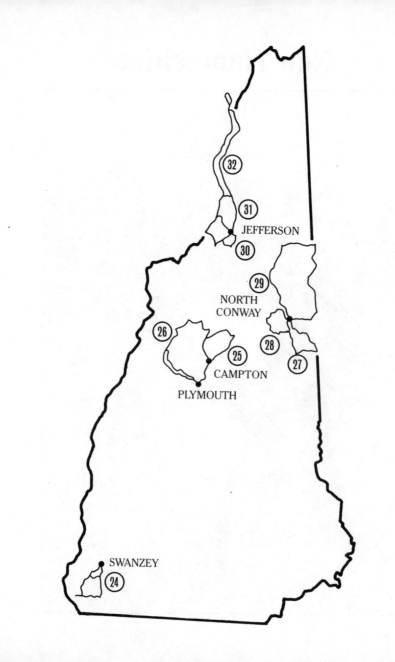

New Hampshire

24

Ashuelot River
Covered Bridge Cruise

Swanzey—Ashuelot—Winchester
Richmond—Swanzey

Everybody loves a covered bridge, except perhaps the truck driver whose rig is too heavy to cross. Cyclists feel a special attraction to these architectural monuments to New England's pioneer days. Covered bridges make us think of how the landscape looked before cars, before bicycles even, when horse-drawn coaches and ox carts provided the primary means of transportation. The tangible bequest of a simpler age, covered bridges provide us with the comforting sense of continuity with our past.

This 36-mile ride passes through five covered bridges as it follows the Ashuelot River running south from Swanzey. The tour follows a triangular course, each leg of which has its own character. The first leg, through the first five bridges, is flat. The second, crossing from Winchester to Richmond, features a difficult 2-mile climb. The third, from Richmond back to Swanzey, is rolling but mostly downhill. A shorter 13-mile option skips the climb and still includes four of the bridges.

The first bridge is just a mile north of the ride's Swanzey starting point. The next three bridges, all built in the early nineteenth century, cross the river within several miles of each other. Each bridge has its own character, varying according to its surrounding landscape and the expense and skill put into its construction.

At 8.5 miles, shortly after you cross the last of these four bridges, the loop turns left onto Old Westport Road. This beautiful, almost forgotten route runs along a fertile but narrow plain between the river and the Pisgah Mountains. Dozens of cows populate the pastures here.

Passing through Winchester, follow the river's elbow west toward the Connecticut River. Although one can continue straight onto the ride's second leg, the finest bridge of all is situated only 3 miles downstream. The Winchester-Ashuelot bridge is neither the state's longest nor its oldest. But its open, unsheathed sides, its red roof, and its siting across a rocky stretch of the Ashuelot make it one of the most beautiful. Photographs of this bridge appear on the covers of more than one tourist guide to New Hampshire. There is a small grocery store here, as well as a nice spot to sit on the opposite side of the river.

Follow a dirt road along the riverbank back to Winchester, then climb eastward out of the Ashuelot's valley. The climb is long and wearying but follows a smooth road and at the top offers a view toward lonely Mount Monadnock.

The Basics

Start: Swanzey, in New Hampshire's southwestern corner, just below Keene. From the Boston area, follow Rte. 119W to Richmond, then follow Rte. 32N to Swanzey. From central Massachusetts and southern New England, follow I-91N through Brattleboro, turn east on Rte. 9 to Keene, then south on routes 12 and 32 to Swanzey. Park in the lots of either the Mount Caesar School or the Monadnock Regional High School, on opposite sides of Rte. 32 at its intersection with Sawyers Crossing Rd.
Length: 12.8 or 35.7 miles.
Terrain: A little bit of everything, including long flat stretches, a little dirt road, and a 2-mile climb.

Food: There is a small grocery store at the covered bridge in Ashuelot, 17.2 miles into the ride and a nice place to stop for a rest on the bank of the river. There are also convenience stores in Winchester, at 15 miles, and at the intersection in Richmond, at 26.2 miles.

Miles & Directions

- 0.0 From the parking lot of either school in Swanzey, ride west on Sawyers Crossing Rd. toward West Swanzey and Keene.
- 0.2 Stay with Sawyers Crossing Rd. as it turns right at the fork.
- 1.0 Pass through first covered bridge over the Ashuelot River and turn left on the other side.
- 1.5 Stay left as Ash Hill Rd. turns right.
- 2.9 Left onto Rte. 10S toward Winchester. Don't let all the barking worry you. That's the Monadnock Regional Humane Society across the street.
- 3.4 Left at blinking light. This is the first possible left on Rte. 10.
- 3.9 Left at T and cross the 1832 Thompsen Covered Bridge, which crosses the Ashuelot River just above a small dam. Continue straight onto Christian Hill Rd. on other side.
- 4.2 Right onto South Grove St. immediately after passing over old railroad bed. Continue straight as another road merges in from the right.
- 5.6 Bear right at junction. Although unmarked, the road to the left is Swanzey Lake Rd.

For a short jaunt totaling 12.8 miles, turn left here and follow Swanzey Lake Rd. for 3.9 miles back to Rte. 32. Pass Swanzey Lake and the turnoff for Richardson Park on the left, or turn in there for a swim, and continue to Rte. 32. Turn left on Rte. 32 back to Swanzey.

- 6.3 Left at stop sign, toward Winchester. But first take a short 0.1-mile detour to the right for a look at the 1862 Slate Bridge, the third covered bridge on this route.

Start/finish in
school parking lot
on Route 32

SWANZEY

TO KEENE

32

covered
bridge

10

Sawyer's Crossing Road

covered
bridge

covered
bridge

South Grove

Swanzey
Lake

covered
bridge

10

Pisgah
State
Park

covered
bridge

36-MILE RIDE

13-MILE

OPTION

Swanzey

Lake Road

Franklin
Mountain

Pisgah
Mountains

Old Westport Road

Old Spafford Road

10

Rattlesnake
Mountain

Franconia
Mountains

32

ASHUELOT

covered
bridge

Elm

WINCHESTER

RICHMOND

Old Ashuelot Road

119

119

10

78

32

N

- 7.1 Left onto Rte. 10S, keeping an eye out for traffic. Ride slowly on Rte. 10, as you will be looking for the first right turn.
- 7.4 Right onto the unmarked road that turns downhill through a cluster of small roadside buildings. This is an easy road to miss, but there is a right turn sign preceding it.
- 7.6 Cross fourth covered bridge and turn left on the other side.
- 8.1 Fork right with the paved road as a dirt road continues straight.
- 8.5 Sharp left at the intersection onto Old Westport Rd. The roads continuing straight and turning left are dirt.
- 13.0 Bear left, staying by the river, as a dirt road joins in from the right.
- 13.5 Turn left onto the unnamed road. This junction is marked by a big red slate-roofed barn on the left.
- 13.8 Straight through intersection toward the rusted-out railroad buildings ahead on the left.
- 14.4 Left toward the iron trestle bridge within sight at the end of Elm St. This is the town of Winchester.
- 4.5 Right onto the narrow road immediately in front of the bridge. Do not cross the river here.

You could continue straight across the bridge here if you wanted to shave 4.4 miles off the total trip distance. Continuing straight, you would cross Rte. 10 in the center of Winchester, with the town hall on your right, and continue onto Rte. 119E toward Richmond. The miles you would miss, though, are among the most scenic of the trip, and the covered bridge at Ashuelot is the grandest along this route.

- 14.7 Bear right with the main road as it turns slightly uphill.
- 15.2 Ride directly across Rte. 119. This back road will drop back down to the Ashuelot River.
- 16.5 Left onto Rte. 119.
- 17.2 Left across the beautifully preserved Winchester-Ashuelot bridge as Rte. 119 veers right.
- 20.1 Left onto Rte. 10N. Then continue through the light at the

intersection. You should now be on combined routes 10 and 119 leading back into Winchester.

- 20.5 Right onto Rte. 119 toward Richmond. This road will climb gradually alongside the appropriately named Roaring Brook. Once the stream and the road diverge, however, the road begins to climb more steeply. The final half mile is the steepest.
- 24.2 Reach top of climb, with a view of Mt. Monadnock straight ahead.
- 26.2 In Richmond, which is little more than a crossroads, turn left onto Rte. 32N toward Swanzey. Rte. 32 is narrow and has no shoulder, but there is very little traffic. The road features several steep drops for the first 5 miles, but it then flattens out for the final run back into Swanzey.
- 35.7 Return to the Mount Caesar School or the Monadnock Regional High School at the junction of Rte. 32 and Sawyers Crossing Rd. in Swanzey.

25

Waterville Valley Challenge

*Campton—Waterville Valley—Thornton
Gap—Woodstock—Campton*

The Waterville Valley Challenge begins at an intersection northeast of Campton from which riders can savor a magnificent view of a bold ring of mountains framing an undisturbed foreground of pond, river, and pines. From Campton the ride follows Route 49 for 9 miles to Waterville Valley. This gradual ascent leads into a round valley formed by nearly thirty peaks; those belong to the Squam Mountains to the south and the White Mountains to the north.

If you choose to ride the complete circuit, then the town of Waterville Valley, a combination of modern skiing mecca and year-round alpine village, signals only that your warm-up climb has ended. Although you will have ascended 1,000 feet in the ride's first 9 miles, you must now brace yourself for an additional climb of 800 feet in the remaining 3 miles to Thornton Gap.

Narrow Tripoli Road leads from the open expanse of the valley into the shadowy interior of a mountainside forest. Passing through Thornton Gap, it crosses the watershed between the Mad and Pemigewasset rivers, following cascading feeder streams of each. There are a number of small campsites and trailheads along this passage. The East Pond and Mount Osceola trails, on the right, cross the Scar Ridge to the Kancamagus Highway.

Take the 7-mile descent from Thornton Gap with your brakes applied. Tripoli Road, paved during the climb, is for the most part well-graded dirt on its downhill side. Be certain that you're riding on sturdy tires, and shout warnings of your approach to hikers along the road.

Many local riders insist that this is one of the best tours in the southern region of the White Mountain National Forest. The Greasy Gonzos, an informal club of the Greasy Wheel bicycle shop in nearby Plymouth, often ride this circuit on their Wednesday evening outings. It's also a favorite ride of employees at the Mountain Valley Bike Shop, at the 11-mile point on the route itself.

A less difficult but still challenging alternative to the full circuit is to ride this as a 23-mile up-and-back route between Campton and Waterville Valley. A third option is simply to drive up to Waterville Valley and knock about on some mountain bikes, possibly including the climb to Thornton Gap in your explorations. Bring your own mountain bikes or rent from the Mountain Valley Bike Shop, which also has maps of local off-road trails.

The Basics

Start: Campton, at the intersections of routes 49 and 175. Take I-93 north to exit 28 for Campton and Waterville Valley. Turn right coming off the exit. Drive one and a half miles on Rte. 49 into town.

Length: 32.1 miles for the complete circuit; 22.8 miles for an up-and-back option.

Terrain: The complete circuit features a gradual 9-mile climb to Waterville Valley along a smooth, broad-shouldered road, followed by a more challenging climb through Thornton Gap along a partially dirt road.

Food: Lunch and snacks are available in Campton, or from the Finish Line and Alpine Pizza restaurants in the town of Waterville Valley, at 10.7 miles.

Miles & Directions

- 0.0 On Rte. 49E in Campton point your bike toward Waterville Valley. Ride toward the mountains, leaving the lake on your right. Gradual climb for the next 9 miles.
- 0.6 Enter White Mountain National Forest.
- 2.6 Stay right on Rte. 49 as it crosses the Mad River.
- 3.2 Pass Sandwich Notch Rd. as it spills down from the right.
- 9.0 Sprint for the sign: "Welcome to Waterville Valley, Incorporated 1829, Population 199." Stay on the main road, Rte. 49, as it becomes Valley Rd. and curves left.
- 10.3 Right on Greeley Rd., toward the cross-country ski center and the Mountain Valley Bike Shop. There should be a golf course on your right and a bicycle path on your left after you complete this turn.
- 10.7 Arrive at the small cluster of buildings at the base of Snow's Mountain. These include the ski center and bike shop, the Finish Line and Alpine Pizza restaurants, and a small equestrian center. After a visit, continue the ride by turning left onto West Branch Rd. The town's small library marks this corner.
- 11.6 West Branch Rd. ends in a T with Tripoli Rd. just after crossing a narrow plank bridge. Turn right here to begin the difficult climb to Thornton Gap and complete the full circuit.

To complete the 22.8-mile option, turn left here and then right onto Rte. 49 in 1.9 miles for the long coast back to Campton.

- 13.7 Tripoli Rd. narrows and turns to well-graded dirt.
- 14.1 Pass through Thornton Gap, 1,800 feet higher in elevation than Campton. Prepare for 7-mile descent along mostly unpaved road.
- 19.2 Pavement begins again and road widens as it passes entrance to Russell Pond Campground.

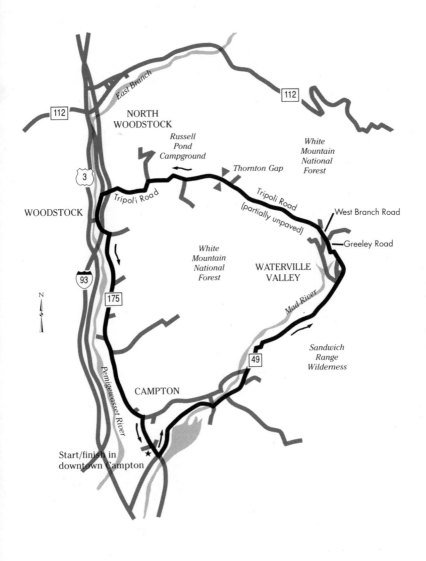

East Branch

112

NORTH
WOODSTOCK

Russell
Pond
Campground

Thornton Gap

White
Mountain
National
Forest

112

3

Tripoli Road

Tripoli Road
(partially unpaved)

West Branch Road

WOODSTOCK

Greeley Road

White
Mountain
National
Forest

WATERVILLE
VALLEY

93

Mad River

175

Sandwich
Range
Wilderness

N

49

Pemigewasset River

CAMPTON

Start/finish in
downtown Campton

- **21.1** Left onto Rte. 175S, toward West Thornton, immediately after passing under I-93.
- **22.6** Stay on Rte. 175S as it takes a right turn and climbs a short, steep hill shortly after passing under I-93 again.
- **32.1** Pass through town of Campton and arrive back at intersection of routes 175 and 49.

26

Kinsman Region Classic

Plymouth—Campton
North Woodstock—Warren
The Rumneys—Plymouth

This challenging, near 60-mile circuit traces a loop around the southwestern corner of New Hampshire's White Mountain National Forest. This is the park's Kinsman Region, named for the notch at its northern reach. It is dominated by four peaks—Mounts Cushman and Kineo, and Carr and Stinson mountains—and bounded by the Pemigewasset and Baker rivers.

The circuit's greatest challenge is its 1,300-foot, 5-mile climb across the watershed between the two rivers. This ascent through dense, unspoiled, and untrafficked forest comes midway, following a long and rolling warm-up stretch from Plymouth to North Woodstock. Two routes are available for the southward stretch home. Both follow the path of the Baker River along the forest's southwestern boundary.

Pedaling easily north from Plymouth, you'll warm up as you pass the small farms and stands of pine along Route 175. Detour to view the covered bridge spanning the Pemigewasset River in the town of Blair, and keep an eye open for the deer that often come down to drink at this spot. From Campton, 5 miles farther along, the view up the Mad River toward Waterville Valley reveals the full mass of the surrounding mountains, their rocky peaks often fading into gray clouds.

Stop for a rest by the bandstand on North Woodstock's town

green, as this route will soon begin a 5.5-mile-long climb toward Kinsman Notch. Be prepared for cooler weather at the top. It would not be unusual, even if you were basking in sunshine during the rest stop in North Woodstock, to find yourself ascending into a mist just a few miles away. In any conditions, the dense forest will soon blot out all sound but that of the brook hidden among the pines to your left. There are several points along this road where you can dismount and rest by the stream. A sweeping 7-mile descent provides ample reward for the effort required by this long, steep climb.

From Warren, you may choose between two parallel routes following the Baker River south toward Plymouth. They rejoin in roughly 17 miles, just short of town. If you want to run a fast pace line in this final stretch, take Option One, which continues along Route 25. This, the valley's principal road, runs slightly downhill, smooth and with a broad shoulder most of the way. It passes through an open, exposed landscape, so before making your choice, consider the direction of the wind. If you feel it in your face, you may prefer Option Two. For a more relaxing ride, turn left onto Oak Hill Road at Warren's southern end. This second route, which changes names several times, traces the edge of the White Mountain National Forest as far as Rumney. Because it parallels the Baker River along its eastern shore, closer to the mountains, it does not offer as flat a course as Route 25. But it does offer less traffic and a generally more tranquil ride.

Visit the Greasy Wheel bicycle shop in Plymouth, home of the Greasy Gonzos bike club, on returning to Plymouth. There you are likely to encounter local riders back from their own rides with whom you can trade stories of adventures encountered along this mountainous route.

The Basics

Start: Plymouth. Take exit 25 off I-93N and turn right on Rte. 175A into Plymouth. Park around the town center's small green.

To park outside the town, turn left off the exit and find a suitable spot near the intersection of routes 175A and 175.

Length: 59.3 or 59.9 miles.

Terrain: Gently rolling hills with one important exception—a serious 5.5-mile climb toward the White Mountain National Forest's Kinsman Notch.

Food: Several choices in North Woodstock, at 23.3 miles, or in Warren, at 39.0 miles.

Miles & Directions

- 0.0 From Plymouth, ride north on combined routes 3 and 25 toward Rumney, Campton, and the White Mountains.
- 0.1 Right onto Rte. 175A toward Holderness.
- 1.0 Left onto Rte. 175N at the Holderness School, toward Campton and Waterville Valley.
- 4.8 Although the tour continues straight, a 1-mile detour to the left on Blair Rd. leads to a 300-foot covered bridge across the Pemigewasset River.
- 6.1 Follow Rte. 175 through the small village of Campton Hollow, shortly after crossing Beebe River.
- 9.0 Cross Mad River and continue on Rte. 175 through Campton. Pass turnoff for Waterville Valley on right.
- 18.5 Left with Rte. 175 at stop sign following a short downhill.
- 21.0 Pemigewasset River parking area on left; pull off for a rest.
- 22.7 Dismount to cross iron grate bridge across Pemigewasset River.
- 22.8 Right at T onto Rte. 3N toward North Woodstock.
- 23.3 Enter North Woodstock, with a view toward Franconia Notch straight ahead and the town green on the right. Turn left onto Rte. 112W toward Woodsville and Lost River. But first you may want to take in the sights and get a bite to eat. Detour to the right on Depot St. to see the covered bridge at Clark's Trading Post.
- 25.9 Left onto Rte. 118 toward Warren as Rte. 112 continues in the direction of Woodsville.

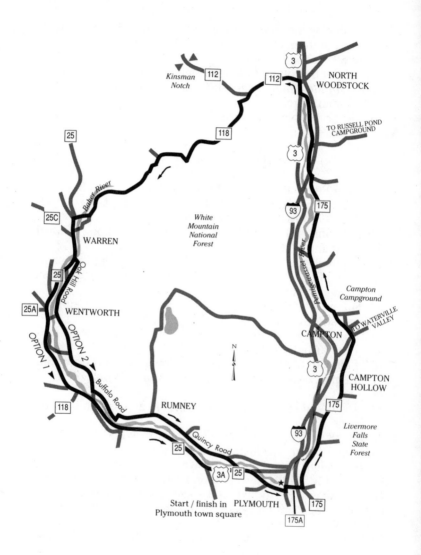

Start / finish in PLYMOUTH
Plymouth town square

- 26.0 Enter White Mountain National Forest and prepare for the climb to begin in earnest.
- 31.5 Top of climb. Sign warns of 7 percent grade for next 3 miles; prepare for total descent of over 7 miles.
- 38.9 Descent ends. Turn south toward Plymouth on combined routes 25E and 118S. Continue straight through Warren.
- 40.4 You may now choose between the two parallel routes following the Baker River south toward Plymouth. Option One continues along Rte. 25, the valley's principal road. Option Two follows secondary and more rolling roads that trace the edge of the White Mountain National Forest as far as Rumney.

Option One

- 40.4 Continue straight on Rte. 25S, passing Bud's Country Store on the left. Keep in mind that you may cross over to the Baker River's eastern side and join the secondary route detailed below by taking any of five left turns in the next 11 miles.
- 47.9 Straight on Rte. 25S as Rte. 118 turns off to the right.
- 55.3 Take second right turn through traffic circle, onto combined routes 3A-E and 25E toward Plymouth.
- 57.2 Right, following sign toward Plymouth downtown.
- 59.3 Arrive at Plymouth town green, at intersection with combined routes 3 and 25.

Option Two

- 40.4 From Rte. 25S turn left onto Oak Hill Rd. at Bud's Country Store on the left. This turn occurs in just less than a mile after your second crossing of the Baker River. You crossed the river once just before turning left onto Rte. 25 and again in Warren. If you have missed this turn, take the next left, East Side Rd., just before crossing the river for a third time.

- 43.4 Stay left at intersection in Wentworth. As a rule, the right turns along this stretch lead back to Rte. 25.
- 48.9 Left onto Buffalo Rd. There is a small cemetery at this intersection.
- 52.4 Straight through Rumney as Buffalo Rd. turns to Quincy Rd. The left turn here leads to the house of Mary Baker Eddy, founder of the Christian Science movement, and then climbs toward Stinson Lake.
- 56.5 Turn right, shortly after passing the small Plymouth Airport, and cross the covered bridge.
- 57.3 Left onto combined routes 25 and 3A-E toward Plymouth.
- 57.8 Turn right, following sign toward Plymouth downtown.
- 59.9 Arrive at Plymouth town green.

27

Crystal Lake Ramble

*North Conway—Conway—Eaton Center
Snowville—West Brownfield
Center Conway—North Conway*

Of the three rides starting and ending in North Conway, this 34-mile meander to Crystal Lake, into Maine, and back provides the most relaxed tour. The Bear Notch Challenge is not much longer but features a long and spectacular climb up to the Kancamagus Highway. And the White Mountain Triple Notch Classic is for experienced cyclists only. By contrast, anybody in good shape should feel comfortable tackling this tour.

The Crystal Lake Ramble explores a wooded no-man's-land between the more bustling White Mountains to the north and the Lake Region to the south. The scenery is not grand, in the sense that the views from Evans Notch or across Lake Winnipesaukee are; it is more intimate. The roads are narrow, the hills small, and the lakes comparatively tiny.

West Side Road, the back route from North Conway to Conway, provides as good a flat warm-up stretch for this ride as it does a cool-down route at the end of the Bear Notch Challenge. Beyond Conway, Route 153 parallels a brook on its way south. The road's ups and downs are slight.

The ride's initial destination is Crystal Lake, the jewel in a chain of a half dozen near-ponds strung from Conway to Ossipee. New Hampshire's largest lakes, Winnipesaukee and Squam, are more famous and more visited. But the hundreds of little lakes like this are far more representative of New Hampshire as a whole. Crystal Lake has its small village, Eaton Center, with a general store or two where cyclists stop for snacks. Children and adults swim from the lake's rocks in summer and drop a line through the ice, waiting for a trout to bite, in winter. Couples are married in the white church on the lake shore. A road circles one side, offering glimpses of these scenes of village life.

For an easy 26-mile outing, return from Crystal Lake along Route 153 and West Side Road back to North Conway. The full Ramble, though, turns toward Maine on Brownfield Road, which rolls and twists, more or less successfully making its way around rather than over many small hills. A couple miles short of Brownfield, Maine, Center Conway Road turns left, leading back to the bustle of North Conway itself.

The Basics

Start: Take Rte. 16 to North Conway. The ride to Crystal Lake takes off from the same point as the tougher Bear Notch and White Mountain Triple Notch tours. Start in the center of North Conway, where Rte. 16 and River Rd. meet. This intersection is on the northern side of the Conway Scenic Railroad station, just half a block from the Eastern Slopes Inn, the Eastern Mountain Sports Shop, and the Joe Jones bicycle and outdoors emporium. During the crowded summer and fall foliage seasons, you may find it easier to park on West Side Rd., just over a mile into the ride.

Length: 34.0 miles for the complete loop or 26.0 miles for a ride to Crystal Lake and back on the same route.

Terrain: This tour through gently rolling forestland follows the relatively flat paths of local rivers and brooks. A few gradual climbs offer some challenge.

Food: Several stores at the intersection of routes 16, 113, and

153 in Conway offer snacks and sandwiches. Best to pack a snack to enjoy by the side of Crystal Lake.

Miles & Directions

- 0.0 From the Conway Scenic Railroad station in the center of North Conway, ride west on River Rd., passing beneath the railroad bridge. Cross the Saco River and continue toward Echo Lake State Park.
- 0.9 Turn left onto West Side Rd., toward White Horse Ledge and Echo Lake State Park, coming across the river.
- 7.4 Continue straight across combined routes 16 and 113 onto Rte. 153. This intersection marks the center of Conway. Last stores until Crystal Lake. Rte. 153 follows a brook toward Crystal Lake and Eaton Center.
- 12.7 Left onto Brownfield Rd. immediately on reaching Crystal Lake. This road is probably unmarked, although a sign here points to Snowville and Brownfield, Maine. Detour to the right for a visit to the lakeside village of Eaton Center.

Return along the same route to complete a shorter 26-mile out-and-back ride.

- 15.0 Stay with Brownfield Rd. over a gradual climb into Maine. In another couple of miles, continue straight through West Brownfield, now on Eaton Center Rd., toward Brownfield.
- 20.1 Left onto Center Conway Rd., as River Rd. curves right. Both are probably unmarked. A white house with a red roof marks the intersection. Follow this road straight through the four corners of South Conway and around the eastern edge of Conway Lake to Rte. 302 in Center Conway. The road changes names to South Conway Rd. and Mill St. along the way.
- 27.8 Left onto Rte. 302W toward North Conway. Ride with caution along this stretch of busy road.
- 29.1 Turn right with combined routes 113 and 302 toward North Conway as Rte. 113 continues straight to Conway.

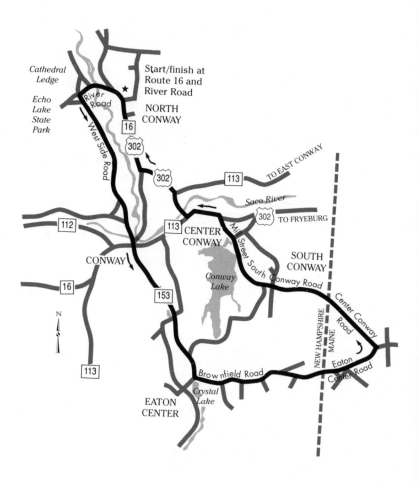

Cathedral
Ledge

Echo
Lake
State
Park

Start/finish at
Route 16 and
River Road

River Road

West Side Road

16

302

302

302

113

TO EAST CONWAY

Saco River

302 TO FRYEBURG

112

113

CENTER
CONWAY

NORTH
CONWAY

CONWAY

16

153

Conway
Lake

Mill Street South Conway Road

SOUTH
CONWAY

Center Conway Road

NEW HAMPSHIRE
MAINE

Eaton
Center Road

N

113

Brownfield Road

EATON
CENTER

Crystal
Lake

- 30.0 Continue straight as Rte. 113, East Conway Rd., turns right toward East Conway and Chatham, Maine.
- 31.7 Right onto Rte. 16N. Ride with caution through this strip of factory outlet malls. This section of road is choked with traffic during most weekends of the year. Keep a sharp eye out for drivers turning in and out of the parking lots on either side.
- 34.0 Return to intersection of Rte. 16 and River Rd., just north of the Conway Scenic Railway station.

28

Bear Notch Challenge

*North Conway—Bartlett—Bear Notch
Quint—North Conway*

Its two lanes arcing over the mountains, the Kancamagus Highway is considered by thousands the ultimate White Mountain road. It stretches 34 miles from the Pemigewasset River at Lincoln to the Saco River at Conway. En route it climbs to nearly 3,000 feet as it crosses the flank of Mount Kancamagus.

On a summer weekend afternoon, dozens of cyclists and hundreds of cars will share the steep and twisting roadway. Once a year, heads turn as the Granite State Wheelmen's annual Tandem Rally cruises by—ten bikes, each driven by four legs instead of two.

To catch some of the action without being overcome by the crowds and cars, try this ride from North Conway through Bear Notch. It follows the route of an annual citizens' race sponsored by the local Joe Jones bicycle and outdoors shop. Riding the course without worrying how you place, you have the opportunity to explore or view the many scenic areas along the way.

Start with a side trip into Echo Lake State Park at one and a half miles into the ride. Here Cathedral Ledge towers 1,000 feet above the Saco River valley. Farther north, on West Side Road, look for Humphrey's Ledge, a steep ridgeside, to your left.

On the long but gradual climb through Bear Notch, don't hesitate to pull off at the four scenic overlooks along the way. Bear Notch Road climbs from 600 to 2,000 feet in approximately

5 miles, so you'll welcome the chance to catch your breath. Bear Mountain itself, rising to the left of the climb, is over 3,200 feet high.

Once on the Kancamagus, if the ride through Bear Notch hasn't been enough for one day, you can detour to the west, uphill, to the Pemi and Kancamagus overlooks. Kancamagus Pass lies just over 8 miles distant and 1,500 feet up. On the return along Route 112, stop at the Rocky Gorge Scenic Area and the Lower Falls Swimming and Picnic Area to view the Swift River's rapids.

Don't forget to turn left through the covered bridge onto Dugway Road, following the signs to the Covered Bridge Campground. Dugway Road runs parallel to the Kancamagus until both end near the junction of the Swift and Saco rivers. From there, West Side Road offers an attractive and completely flat alternative to Route 16 (North Conway's strip of factory outlet malls) for the ride back into town.

This is an extraordinarily rewarding ride, challenging enough for the experienced cyclist while suitable for those with a more leisurely tour in mind.

The Basics

Start: In the center of North Conway, where Rte. 16 and River Rd. meet. This intersection is on the northern side of the Conway Scenic Railroad station, just half a block from the Eastern Slopes Inn, the Eastern Mountain Sports Shop, and the Joe Jones bicycle and outdoors emporium. During the crowded summer and fall seasons, you may find it easier to park on West Side Rd., just over a mile into the ride.

Length: 37.7 miles.

Terrain: Rivers and mountain. Includes both quiet valley roads and a 1,400-foot climb in 5 miles through Bear Notch.

Food: Pack a snack to enjoy during a rest at any of several overlooks and picnic areas on Bear Notch Road and the Kancamagus Highway.

Miles & Directions

- **0.0** From the Conway Scenic Railroad station in the center of North Conway, ride west on River Rd., passing beneath the railroad bridge. Cross the Saco River and continue toward Echo Lake State Park and Cathedral Ledge.
- **0.9** Stay right coming across the river, merging into West Side Rd.
- **1.5** Stay right with West Side Rd., which follows the Saco River north.
- **6.5** Left onto Rte. 302W, toward Attitash Ski Area and Bartlett.
- **10.5** Left onto Bear Notch Rd. at the blinking red light in Bartlett and cross the Maine Central Railroad tracks.
- **11.0** Gradually begin climb toward Bear Notch. Stay on the main road, avoiding the secondary turnoffs to the right.
- **19.6** Left at the end of Bear Notch Rd. onto the Kancamagus Highway, Rte. 112.
- **25.4** Left, crossing the covered bridge spanning the Swift River, and then right onto Dugway Rd.
- **31.8** Take the first left after crossing the railroad tracks.
- **32.1** Take the next left onto West Side Rd. back toward Echo Lake State Park and North Conway.
- **37.2** Pass the entrance to Echo Lake State Park on the left.
- **37.7** Right onto River Rd. back toward Conway.
- **36.8** Right to cross Saco River.
- **37.7** Return to Rte. 16 in North Conway center.

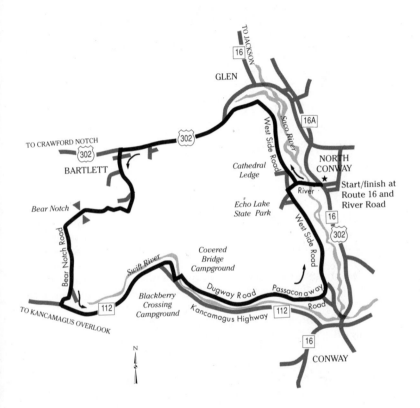

TO JACKSON

16

GLEN

302

TO CRAWFORD NOTCH

302

BARTLETT

West Side Road

Saco River

16A

Cathedral
Ledge

NORTH
CONWAY

★ Start/finish at
Route 16 and
River Road

River

Bear Notch

Echo Lake
State Park

West Side Road

16
302

Bear Notch Road

Swift River

Covered
Bridge
Campground

Dugway Road

Passaconaway Road

TO KANCAMAGUS OVERLOOK

112

Blackberry
Crossing
Campground

Kancamagus Highway

112

16

N

CONWAY

29

White Mountain
Triple Notch Classic

---

*North Conway—South Chatham—Stow
Evans Notch—Gilead—Gorham
Pinkham Notch—Glen—North Conway*

New Hampshire's White Mountain National Forest is a serious cyclist's dream come true. Here smooth highways pass through glacial mountain passes and wind along unspoiled rural valleys, revealing new vistas at every turn. Hikers, campers, rock climbers, river runners, and cyclists alike consider this their recreational paradise. And in these three-quarters of a million acres is enough room for everybody—even if it may not seem that way in downtown North Conway, the region's gateway town, during the peak summer season.

The Triple Notch Classic will lead you deep into cool conifer forests far from the factory outlet stores of North Conway. The tour circles past or through some of the most notable landmarks in the White Mountain region: Hurricane Mountain; Evans and Pinkham notches; the Great Gulf Wilderness area; Mount Washington; and the village of Jackson with its humble covered bridge. This 75-mile circuit is the most difficult of this book's three North Conway–based rides. It should be ridden by experienced cyclists only.

The Triple Notch Classic and the shorter Bear Notch Challenge and Crystal Lake Ramble are favorites of the Granite State

---

Wheelmen, New Hampshire's largest cycling club. Every year more than 50 of the club's 1,200 members meet in North Conway for the late summer Mount Washington Valley Weekend to ride these and other tours. They stay in the Cranmore Mountain Lodge, although Conway and the surrounding villages also abound with small inns and bed and breakfast operations catering to an outdoor crowd. Plan a weekend of your own; mix cycling with hiking, swimming, or just lying about, which is all you may feel like doing after conquering this tour's climbs.

The three climbs of the Triple Notch Classic are Hurricane Mountain and the more gradual and smooth Evans and Pinkham notches. If you feel like limiting your day's cycling exploits to two climbs instead of three, you may avoid the wildly beautiful but severe climb up Hurricane Mountain Road by circling to the south. Directions for an alternate starting route, around Hurricane and neighboring Black Cap mountains, are presented at the end of the principal directions below.

Once over or around Hurricane Mountain, the route rolls gently along the state's border with Maine toward Evans Notch. After passing the Cold River Campground you will climb steadily through a white birch forest. Four miles later, stop at the Evans Notch Overlook to count the peaks around you. The next 8 miles will pass in a blur as the road careens through a winding canyon to the Androscoggin River below.

Cycle through Pinkham Notch slowly, as there is much to see here. Pull off the road at the scenic turnout for the Great Gulf Wilderness area. A sign here names the peaks of the Presidential Range before you.

The Classic passes by the entrance to the Mount Washington Auto Road. This toll road is open to bicycles one day every year for the Mount Washington Hillclimb, a fierce race to its peak. The road ascends 4,000 feet in 8 twisting miles. Much of it is unpaved. The weather near the summit is notoriously unpredictable and harsh—in 1934 observatory instruments on the summit recorded the greatest wind speed ever documented on the planet, 231 miles per hour. These factors combine to endow this race with its reputation as the toughest mountain time trial in the country. The fastest time ever posted is just short of one hour.

Rather than climb this hill, then, stop at the rustic Appalachian Mountain Club lodge in Pinkham Notch instead. There is a small cafe here, as well as a large lounge area and a bookstore with dozens of volumes about the surrounding wilderness. The Classic's remaining 20 miles are virtually all downhill or flat. The road passes from wilderness into condominium territory, with a scenic stop in the village of Jackson in between.

The Basics

Start: In the center of North Conway, at the junction of combined routes 16 and 302 with Kearsarge Rd. This intersection is opposite the Conway Scenic Railroad station, next to the Joe Jones bicycle, ski, and outdoors shop and just half a block south of the Eastern Slopes Inn and Eastern Mountain Sports shop.
Length: 74.5 miles, or 81.1 miles with alternate route around Hurricane Mountain.
Terrain: Features three major climbs—over Hurricane Mountain and Evans and Pinkham notches—each with elevation gains of over 1,200 feet. But you will also enjoy two rewarding 8-mile-long descents. The alternate route avoids Hurricane Mountain and offers a more gentle warm-up to the ride.
Food: Appalachian Mountain Club lodge in Pinkham Notch at 54.4 or 61.0 miles. Small grocery stores on the route in Stow, Shelburne, and Gorham.

Miles & Directions

- 0.0 From Rte. 16 in North Conway, ride east on Kearsarge Rd. toward the Cranmore Mountain ski area.
- 0.5 Turn left with Kearsarge Rd., continuing past the Sunnyside Inn and toward Cranmore Mountain.

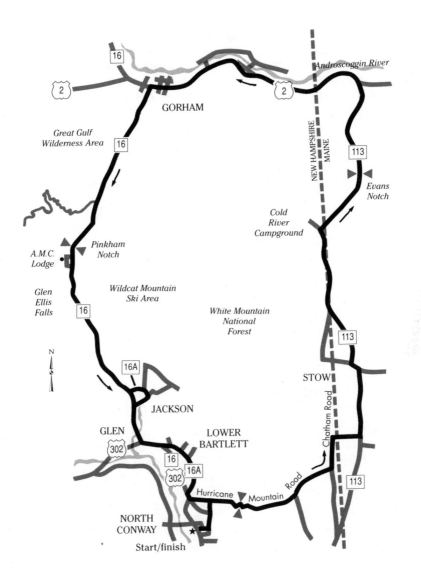

16

2

Androscoggin River

GORHAM

Great Gulf
Wilderness Area

16

NEW HAMPSHIRE
MAINE

113

Evans
Notch

Cold
River
Campground

A.M.C.
Lodge

Pinkham
Notch

Glen
Ellis
Falls

16

Wildcat Mountain
Ski Area

White Mountain
National
Forest

113

N

16A

STOW

Chatham Road

JACKSON

GLEN

LOWER
BARTLETT

302

16

302 16A

113

Hurricane   Mountain   Road

NORTH
CONWAY

★

Start/finish

- **2.0** Right onto Hurricane Mountain Rd. at the end of Kearsarge Rd., soon after passing the Cranmore Mountain Lodge on the right. Severe climb over Hurricane Mountain, beginning in just over 1 mile, should be ridden easily as a warm-up.
- **6.0** Hurricane Mountain Rd. bottoms out at Chatham Rd. Turn left.
- **11.2** Chatham Rd. ends at T in North Fryeburg, Maine. Turn left on Rte. 113N toward Chatham and North Chatham.
- **14.0** Right with Rte. 113N toward North Chatham and Gilead at Gulf station and Stow Corner Store on left.
- **17.1** Continue straight, crossing back into New Hampshire, as Rte. 113B merges in from left.
- **21.6** Enter White Mountain National Forest. Begin climb to Evans Notch shortly after passing into Maine again.
- **23.9** Cold River Overlook on the right.
- **24.3** Climb ends at Evans Notch Overlook. Begin 8.2-mile descent.
- **32.5** Descent ends. Turn left at stop onto Rte. 2W toward Gorham.
- **44.4** In Gorham, turn left on Rte. 16S toward Conway and Mt. Washington Auto Road. Climb to Pinkham Notch begins gradually.
- **52.2** Reach Great Gulf Wilderness Area scenic overlook on right.
- **54.8** End of climb. Appalachian Mountain Club lodge on right. Prepare for 10-mile descent to Jackson village and Glen; 9 percent grade for next 3 miles.
- **64.1** Pass the turnoff to the left for Rte. 16A. For a scenic 1-mile detour, turn left here—Rte. 16A is also Jackson Village Rd.—directly opposite the Exxon station. Follow this road as it curves to the right through Jackson village and the Jackson covered bridge before rejoining Rte. 16S.
- **66.1** Continue on Rte. 16S through traffic circle in Glen.
- **67.3** Left, crossing Rte. 16 with care, onto Rte. 16A, Intervale resort loop, to avoid the busy main road into town.
- **70.3** Turn left as 16A merges back into Rte. 16.
- **70.5** Left onto Hurricane Mountain Rd.

- 72.5 Right onto Kearsarge Rd., toward the Cranmore Mountain Lodge. Follow Kearsarge Rd. back to Rte. 16 in North Conway center.
- 74.5 Arrive back at combined routes 16 and 302 in North Conway.

Alternate Starting Route

This alternate route avoids Hurricane Mountain by adding 6.6 completely flat miles to the tour's total distance. But you must ride through North Conway's strip of factory outlet malls along Rte. 16, which is choked with traffic during most weekends of the year. Ride cautiously, keeping a sharp eye out for drivers turning in and out of the parking lots on either side. Within 5 miles you will enter the rural farmscape of the Saco River plain.

- 0.0 ride south on combined routes 16 and 302 from the junction with Kearsarge Rd. in North Conway.
- 2.2 Left onto Rte. 302E toward Center Conway, East Conway, and Fryeburg, Maine. Rte. 16 continues straight here.
- 3.9 Left onto Rte. 113, East Conway Rd., toward East Conway and Chatham, Maine.
- 9.5 Stay left at junction. A granite pillar in the intersection here indicates that this is East Conway. The road to the right leads to Fryeburg, Maine.
- 10.3 Bear left onto Green Hill Rd. as Rte. 113 curves right toward West Fryeburg.
- 13.6 Continue straight through intersection onto Chatham Rd. as Hurricane Mountain Rd. comes down from the left. You have now completed the detour around Hurricane Mountain. Continue with the directions above starting at 6.0 miles.

30

Cherry Mountain Ramble

Jefferson—Jefferson Highland—Meadows
Whitefield—Jefferson

The Cherry Mountain Ramble explores the pocket of land that lies between the Pilot Region and the main body of the White Mountain National Forest. This is relatively flat terrain. It is laced by the streams that run off the mountains to the west—Haystack Mountain, Mounts Starr and Waumbeck, Mount Martha, Cherry Mountain, and Beech Hill—on their way to the Connecticut River.

This 28-mile tour is intended as a companion ride to the Grand Groveton Challenge or the Canada and Back Downhill Classic. It is perfect for working the kinks out of your legs in anticipation of the next day's big ride. You could shave off a few miles, and make this an even more relaxing outing, by pedaling directly south from Jefferson on Route 115A and joining Route 115 at Jefferson Station.

The Cherry Mountain Ramble is short enough to allow time to visit the Jefferson area's two tourist attractions. Santa's Village, near the intersection of routes 2 and 16 in Jefferson, is where St. Nick and his entourage of reindeer and helpers spend their summers. Six Gun City, at the junction of routes 2 and 115, is an out-of-place replica of a small western town. If you're tired of pedaling, take a stagecoach ride past the blockhouse, jail, and saloon. Having children along is likely to enhance your enjoyment of these two sites.

The Basics

Start: Jefferson, located on Rte. 2, just southeast of Lancaster and southwest of the White Mountain National Forest's Pilot Region. Follow either I-91N along the Vermont–New Hampshire border or I-93N through New Hampshire. From I-91, turn south onto I-93 in St. Johnsbury, cross into New Hampshire, then take Rte. 116N to Jefferson. Driving north on I-93, follow Rte. 116N to Jefferson.

Length: 28.0 miles.

Terrain: Rolling foothills of the White Mountains.

Food: Pack your own, or stop for a snack in Whitefield.

Miles & Directions

- 0.0 From the center of Jefferson, at the intersection of routes 2 and 115A, ride east on Rte. 2. (You could take a shortcut and ride directly south on Rte. 115A, through Jefferson Station, to Rte. 115S.)
- 4.1 Turn right onto Rte. 115S toward Meadows and Jefferson Station, circling the western base of Cherry Mountain.
- 12.1 Cut over to Rte. 3 by turning right onto Lennon Rd. before reaching the junction of routes 115 and 3 in Carroll. Enjoy the long coasting stretch!
- 13.9 Turn right onto Rte. 3 toward Whitefield.
- 18.8 In Whitefield, take two successive right turns to get onto Rte. 116N, Jefferson Rd., to Jefferson. Be certain not to detour onto one of the secondary roads. Stay with Rte. 116 all the way to Rte. 2.
- 27.5 Turn right onto Rte. 2E.
- 28.0 Arrive in Jefferson.

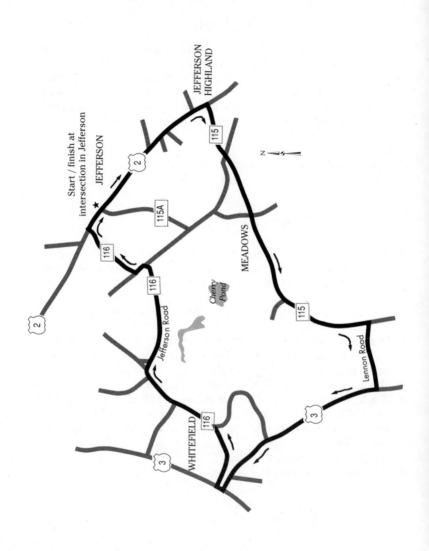

31

Grand Groveton Challenge

The Grand Groveton Challenge can be either a substitute for or companion ride to the Canada and Back Downhill Classic. Or combine both with the shorter Cherry Hill Ramble for a full three days of cycling through New Hampshire's north country. The Grand Groveton Challenge qualifies as a metric century ride, one that covers a distance of 100 kilometers, or 62 miles.

All three rides are the contribution of Adolphe Bernotas, who organized the first ride to Canada for his club, the Granite State Wheelmen, in 1979. Since then very little about this countryside has changed. Jefferson and the surrounding region lie far enough north to have avoided the development that has brought both prosperity and traffic to the state's southern fringe.

This is the ultimate ride from Jefferson. It combines covered bridges, sensational downhills, flat stretches along the Connecticut River, and quaint Yankee villages with open views, vistas, and panoramas in abundance. In short, you will see much of the best of New England within a manageable 64 miles. If there is a single highlight to the tour it is the village of Stark, west of Groveton on the Ammonoosuc River, where a covered bridge and a traditional New England church nestle side by side in the shadow of sheer granite cliffs.

The Basics

Start: Jefferson, located on Rte. 2, just southeast of Lancaster and southwest of the White Mountain National Forest's Pilot Region. Follow either I-91N along the Vermont–New Hampshire border or I-93N through New Hampshire. From I-91, turn south onto I-93 in St. Johnsbury, cross into New Hampshire, then take Rte. 116N to Jefferson. Driving north on I-93, follow Rte. 116N to Jefferson.
Length: 64 miles.
Terrain: Rolling landscape of hills and valleys with many long flat stretches.
Food: Your choice of general stores in Stark, Groveton, or Lancaster. If you are packing a lunch, the Guildhall green at 34.3 miles is a nice midway point to stop for a picnic.

Miles & Directions

- 0.0 The Grand Groveton Challenge follows the same route as the Canada and Back Downhill Classic as far as Groveton. From the center of Jefferson, at the intersection of routes 2 and 115A, ride west on Rte. 2 toward Lancaster.
- 0.8 Right onto North Rd. Stay left at the next fork, as Gore Rd. turns right.
- 5.8 Right on Grange Rd., at the H (hospital) sign toward Grange, Lost Nation, and Groveton. You have missed this turn if you enter Lancaster. Follow Grange Rd. all the way to Groveton.
- 17.0 In Groveton, turn right onto Rte. 110, passing between the Canadian National Railway line and the Ammonoosuc River on the way to Stark.
- 23.2 In Stark, turn left onto Emerson Rd., the back road back to Groveton, crossing the Ammonoosuc.
- 26.7 Left at fork at small cemetery on left.
- 27.5 Stay to the right, continuing along the northern bank of the river, as another road forks to the left across it.

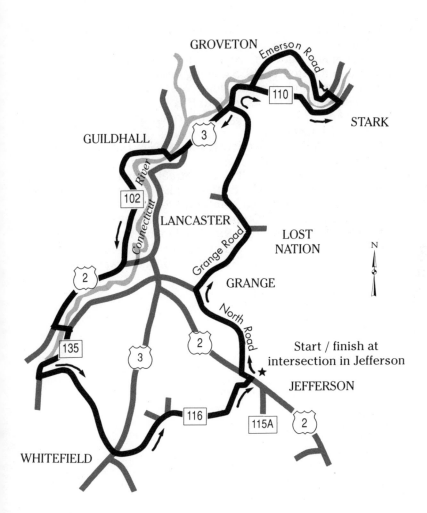

GROVETON

Emerson Road

110

STARK

GUILDHALL

3

River

102

Connecticut

LANCASTER

Grange Road

LOST
NATION

2

GRANGE

North Road

135

3

2

Start / finish at
intersection in Jefferson

JEFFERSON

116

115A

2

WHITEFIELD

N

- 30.5 Left onto Rte. 3S, recrossing the Ammonoosuc, to Northumberland.
- 33.3 Bear right at the shopping center, following the signs to Vermont, as you enter the small town of Northumberland.
- 34.0 Sharp right across the bridge into Guildhall, Vermont.
- 34.3 Left onto Rte. 102S coming off the bridge.
- 41.4 Continue straight along western side of Connecticut River as Rte. 102 merges into Rte. 2.
- 45.3 Left at fork, staying by the river, as Rte. 2 turns inland toward Lunenburg.
- 45.8 Cross the Connecticut River into New Hampshire through the covered bridge.
- 46.0 Right onto Rte. 135S, Elm Street, coming off the bridge.
- 49.0 Left, inland, toward Whitefield. This is the first clear left turn since you turned south on Rte. 135. It comes immediately before Rte. 135 crosses a set of railroad tracks.
- 54.9 In Whitefield, cross Rte. 3 and follow Rte. 116N, Jefferson Rd., to Jefferson. Be certain not to detour onto one of the secondary roads. Stay with Rte. 116 all the way to Rte. 2.
- 63.6 Right onto Rte. 2E.
- 64.1 Arrive in Jefferson.

32

Canada and Back
Downhill Classic

Jefferson—Grange—Groveton
Colebrook—West Stewartstown
Canaan—Quebec—Canaan—Bloomfield
Guildhall—Lancaster—Jefferson

Few visitors to New Hampshire venture farther north than the Lakes Region and White Mountain National Forest. These areas alone hold enough natural wonders and scenery to satisfy repeat vacationers year after year. Beyond the northern slopes of the Presidential Range, where the body of the state begins to narrow, lie untrafficked roads and an undeveloped, pastoral land. And beyond that lies Canada—which brings us to the Canada and Back Downhill Classic.

This 100-mile "century" ride starts in the northern White Mountain town of Jefferson and has as its ultimate destination the "Welcome to Quebec" sign at the U.S.–Canadian border. To get there, the tour follows the Connecticut River valley northward through New Hampshire. The return trip southward through Vermont takes roads that travel directly alongside the river itself.

This route features a roughly 20-mile extension that qualifies it for double-metric status (100 kilometers times two). Besides giving you a chance actually to see some of Quebec instead of just turning around at its border, the extra distance will grant you bragging rights over those who consider a 100-mile century the ultimate cycling achievement.

Don't let fear of New Hampshire–sized hills scare you off. In the words of Adolphe Bernotas, who first mapped out this route for the Granite State Wheelmen, "A combination of geological, geographical and highway engineering vicissitudes make most of this outstanding ride downhill." In fact, the ride's only real climb occurs in its final 8 miles, the home stretch back to Jefferson.

Known to the Granite State Wheelmen as the International Century, this ride is now a keystone event of what has become one of the club's most popular cycling weekends, held every year around July 4. In 1979, the event's first year, fewer than a dozen riders showed up for the 6:30 A.M. start. In its most recent runnings, more than five times that number have ridden at least one of the dozen routes mapped out for the three-day event.

The growing popularity of the International Century weekend has forced the Granite State Wheelmen to move its base camp to Lancaster, which offers more facilities. But for the sake of authenticity, and for a long downhill run to speed you on your way, Adolphe recommends following the ride's original route from and back to Jefferson.

If you can't join the Granite State Wheelmen next July Fourth weekend, why not plan your own weekend on wheels? Choose from the Canada and Back Downhill Classic, its double-metric cousin, and the shorter Cherry Mountain and Grand Groveton rides.

The Basics

Start: Jefferson, located on Rte. 2, just southeast of Lancaster and southwest of the White Mountain National Forest's Pilot Region. Follow either I-91N along the Vermont–New Hampshire border or I-93N through New Hampshire. From I-91, turn south onto I-93 in St. Johnsbury, cross into New Hampshire, then take

Rte. 116N to Jefferson. Driving north on I-93, follow Rte. 116N to Jefferson.

Length: 108 or 128 miles to reach Canada, with shorter options of 47, 64, 80, or 90 miles.

Terrain: Virtually flat or downhill—except for the last 8 miles.

Food: McKenzie's, just north of Groteton, New Hampshire, at 15 miles, is the traditional breakfast stop. Solomon's Store, in West Stewartstown, New Hampshire, is a source for snacks to eat at the bandstand across the street. For those riding the double metric century into Quebec, Motel Montagnard is a good place for sandwiches.

Miles & Directions

- 0.0 From the center of Jefferson, at the intersection of routes 2 and 115A, ride west on Rte. 2 toward Lancaster.
- 0.8 Right onto North Rd. Stay left at the next fork, as Gore Rd. turns right.
- 5.8 Right on Grange Rd., at the H (hospital) sign toward Grange, Lost Nation, and Groveton. You have missed this turn if you enter Lancaster. Follow Grange Rd. all the way to Groveton.
- 17.0 Either cross the covered bridge, which is closed to automobile traffic, or turn left on Rte. 110 and then immediately right onto Rte. 3N. McKenzie's, the Granite State Wheelmen's traditional breakfast stop, follows on the left. Continue on Rte. 3N for 34 miles to West Stewartstown.
- 23.0 Continue through Stratford.

Here is your first chance to turn back. Cross the Connecticut River toward Maidstone, Vermont, and turn left onto Rte. 102S in 0.7 miles. Skip to directions at 99.3 miles below, for a round trip of 46.8 miles.

- 31.0 Pass through North Stratford.

Second chance to turn back. Cross river to Bloomfield, Vermont, and turn left onto Rte. 102S in 0.1 miles. Pick

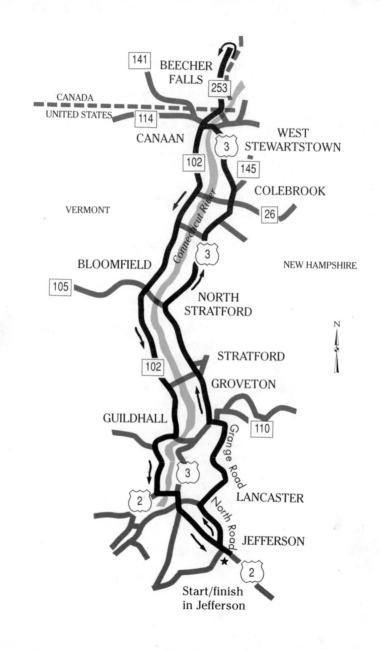

141

BEECHER
FALLS

253

CANADA

UNITED STATES

114

CANAAN

WEST
STEWARTSTOWN

3

102

145

COLEBROOK

26

VERMONT

Connecticut River

3

BLOOMFIELD

NEW HAMPSHIRE

105

NORTH
STRATFORD

STRATFORD

102

GROVETON

GUILDHALL

110

Grange Road

3

2

LANCASTER

North Road

JEFFERSON

2

★

Start/finish
in Jefferson

N

up directions at 76.5 miles below, for a round trip of 63.6 miles.

■ 40.0 Pass through Columbia, staying on Rte. 3N.

Third turnaround point. Cross through covered bridge to Lemington, Vermont, and turn left onto Rte. 102S in 0.8 miles. Continue with directions below starting at 76.5 miles, for a round trip of 79.9 miles.

■ 44.2 Continue on Rte. 3N through Colebrook.

Fourth and last chance to turn around before you might as well complete the entire ride. Cross river, again toward Lemington, Vermont, and turn south on Rte. 102 in 1.0 miles. Pick up directions below at 76.5 miles, for a round trip of 90.6 miles.

■ 51.0 In West Stewartstown, at the sign for Rte. 114 to Montreal, turn left across the bridge into Canaan, Vermont. Just before the bridge is Solomon's Store, a good place for food. The bandstand across the street from Solomon's and the town green opposite the Gulf station are good spots for a rest.
■ 51.4 Coming off the bridge, turn right onto Rte. 253 to Beecher Falls.
■ 53.3 Left for the border at the blinking light in Beecher Falls.
■ 53.6 Stop for customs, cross international border, and make sure a friend photographs you at the "Quebec" sign. This is the turnaround point for the 108-mile ride. From here, backtrack along Rte. 253 to Canaan.

Those wishing to complete a double metric century—twice 100 kilometers—should stay on Rte. 253N past East Hereford to Saint-Venat-de-Hereford (Paquette). Here, visit the beautiful Notre Dame de la Confiance church before turning around and heading back to the border on Rte. 253S. Continue with the directions below, simply adding 20 miles to the distances noted.

187

- 55.8 Cross Rte. 114 and continue onto Rte. 102S. Follow Rte. 102, which runs parallel to the Connecticut River, for the next 43.5 miles.
- 76.5 Just south of the turnoff for Rte. 105 to the right, stay on Rte. 102 as it turns to dirt for just over 1 mile. (This stretch is likely to be paved soon.)
- 99.3 Left onto Rte. 2E, crossing the Connecticut River to Lancaster.
- 100.2 Merge right, entering Lancaster, onto combined routes 2E and 3S.
- 100.9 Bear left with Rte. 2E toward Jefferson and the White Mountain National Forest immediately after crossing short bridge over Israel River.
- 108.0 Arrive back in Jefferson.

Rhode Island

Rhode Island

33

Newport Cottages
and Countryside Ramble

Newport Harbor—Brenton Point
Middletown—Newport Harbor

The Newport Cottages and Countryside Ramble draws a figure-eight loop around the southern end of Aquidneck Island. The loop's first half follows Ocean Drive around the magnificent shoreline southwest of Newport. The second half passes from Newport's splendor and bustle to the quieter countryside and Yankee charm of the island's southwestern end. The two loops, the first measuring 10 and the second 17 miles long, may be ridden separately or together.

Because Newport is a summer resort and often suffers bumper-to-bumper traffic from June through August, this Ramble is best ridden in the spring or fall. In the off-season you will be able to find a parking spot at King Park, which lines Newport Harbor's southern edge along Wellington Avenue. From there, ride away from town. To complete the first, 10-mile loop, follow the general rule of sticking to the principal roads closest to the shore until you arrive at Bellevue Avenue, which leads back into town.

Detour to the right within the first 2 miles for a side trip to Fort Adams State Park. This granite-walled fort was originally constructed to guard the entrance to Narragansett Bay. Sited on a point of land jutting northward into the water, the fort offers terrific views of Newport Harbor and the Newport Bridge. Continuing toward Brenton Point, the route passes Hammersmith Farm, where Jacqueline and John F. Kennedy spent numerous summer vacations. This estate is open for tours from April through mid-November. Highlights include the shingle-style mansion and bayside gardens designed by Frederick Law Olmsted. Canada geese flock on this old farm's broad pastures every fall.

From the U.S. Coast Guard station at Castle Hill, the ride turns south toward the open sea. Follow Ocean Drive along the rocky, wild shoreline for the next 4 miles. Take the time to explore the many grassy areas, boulders, and tidal pools to the right. If you have packed something to eat, stop along this stretch for a roadside picnic. If the wind is blowing from the south, you are likely to feel some of the salt spray sent flying by waves crashing against the rocks.

Bellevue Avenue is the chain along which Newport's jewels are strung. Many of the town's most famous mansions—Belcourt Castle, Marble Head, Beechwood, Chateau-sur-Mer, and The Elms—line either side. Glancing through the gates as you ride by will help you decide which to tour once your bikes are stowed safely away.

The longer of the two loops along this route explores the quieter countryside northwest of town. Tidy shingled homes, small farms, and vast fields line the back roads between Newport and Middletown. The road through sandy Easton and Sachuest points offers views back to Newport, where the most famous of the town's mansions, The Breakers, is visible above the cliff. Back lanes follow the Sakonnet River's western shore, opposite terrain covered by the Sakonnet River Ramble (which follows this ride), before turning back to Newport.

The Basics

Start: King Park, on the southern side of Newport Harbor. From I-195 out of Providence, follow Rte. 138 into Newport; from the

Boston area, follow Rte. 128 to Rte. 24 to Rte. 79 to Rte. 138. To reach the park, drive (or ride) down the harborfront (Thames St.), then turn right on Wellington Ave. King Park will be on the right.

Length: 27.3 miles for the full figure-eight loop; 10.1 or 17.2 miles for either half.

Terrain: Flat coastal roads. Heavy traffic in summer.

Food: There are no commercial areas along this ocean-side route. Pack a snack to enjoy along the shore.

Miles & Directions

- 0.0 From King Park, ride westward, away from town, along Wellington Ave.
- 0.5 Left with Wellington Ave. as it becomes Halidon Ave.
- 0.8 Right onto Harrison Ave.
- 1.2 Bear right with Harrison Ave.
- 1.7 Pass entrance on right to Fort Adams State Park. The Fort guards the mouth of Newport Harbor. It is worth a quick side trip to view Newport from across the water.
- 3.7 Bear right onto Ridge Rd. as Harrison Ave. turns left.
- 4.4 Right onto Ocean Ave., at T, after passing Castle Hill Coast Guard Station.
- 6.4 Bear right with Ocean Ave. where Brenton Rd. forks left.
- 8.1 Right at the T, then turn left almost immediately onto Bellevue Ave.
- 9.6 Right onto Narragansett Ave. to begin the second loop of this figure-eight route.
  To complete the 10.1-mile option, turn left onto Narragansett and then right onto Marchant St. in three blocks. Marchant St. will end at Bellevue Ave. across from King Park.
- 9.9 Left on Annandale Rd.
- 10.5 Right on Memorial Blvd., Rte. 138A.
- 11.5 Stay right at fork, toward East Point, after passing Newport Beach on the right.
- 11.9 Right on Tuckerman.

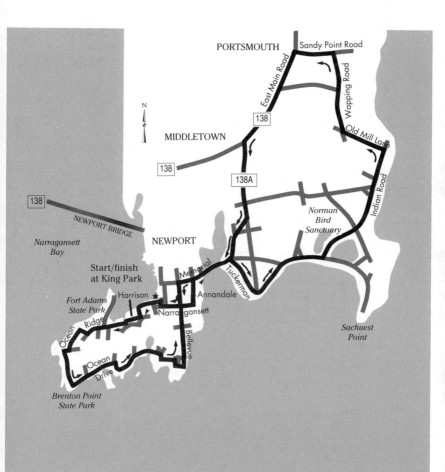

PORTSMOUTH

Sandy Point Road

East Main Road

Wapping Road

138

MIDDLETOWN

Old Mill Lane

138

138A

Indian Road

Norman
Bird
Sanctuary

138

NEWPORT BRIDGE

NEWPORT

Narragansett
Bay

Start/finish
at King Park

Memorial

Tuckerman

Fort Adams
State Park

Harrison

Annandale

Ocean
Ridge

Narragansett

Bellevue

Sachuest
Point

Ocean
Drive

Brenton Point
State Park

- 13.2 Bear right toward the Norman Bird Sanctuary.
- 13.5 Bear left at fork toward the bird sanctuary. You may want to detour to the right for a visit to Sachuest Point, a peninsula of sandy beach marking the mouth of the Sakonnet River.
- 14.8 Cross Third Beach Rd., continuing straight on Indian Road.
- 16.7 Left onto Old Mill Lane where a sign indicates that the road you are on is coming to a dead end.
- 17.4 Right at the T onto Wapping Rd.
- 18.4 Stay right with the fork.
- 19.4 Left at T onto Sandy Point Rd. Sign points left toward Rte. 138.
- 19.9 Left onto Rte. 138 at the stop light. Caution: busy road.
- 22.5 Left onto Rte. 138A, Aquidneck Ave., following the sign for Newport Beach.
- 24.6 Stay with Rte. 138A as it turns left, at a stoplight, and then right, immediately thereafter, toward Newport Beach.
- 26.3 Returning to Newport, turn left off Rte. 138A, Memorial Blvd., onto Bellevue Ave.
- 26.8 Right on Narragansett Ave.
- 27.2 Turn right on Marchant St.
- 27.3 Arrive back at Wellington Ave. and King Park.

34

Sakonnet River Ramble

*Tiverton—Little Compton—Sakonnet Point
Tiverton*

In eastern Rhode Island, country lanes lace the 4-mile-wide strip of salt marshes, farms, and woods lying between the broad Sakonnet River and the Massachusetts border. This is Rhode Island's flatter half; the barely rolling landscape contrasts with the wooded hill and valley country west of Narragansett Bay. This Ramble hugs the Sakonnet River's eastern shore from the town of Tiverton to Sakonnet Point, which juts out into the sea. The route turns inland just long enough to pass through the village of Little Compton, by most accounts the prettiest in the state.

Pedaling past expansive wetlands and pastures, one would never know that this is the nation's most densely populated state. The Narragansett Bay Wheelmen, Rhode Island's largest bicycling club, frequent these roads. Arrows painted on the roads to mark Sunday morning rides still adorn many intersections.

The Ramble starts by following Route 77 south for just a mile and then turning onto back roads toward the Sakonnet River. A small bridge crosses the neck of Nannaquaket Pond. Fishermen often drop their lines here, where the currents carry their hoped-for prey through a narrow channel out to the river. Nannaquaket Road leads past gracious homes situated on a ridge between the two bodies of water.

Another short stretch along Route 77, and the ride turns back toward the river. Neck Road passes through the Seapowet Wildlife Management Area. Great blue herons are often spotted feeding in these wetlands. The course crosses a one-lane wooden bridge over one of the Sakonnet River's many tidal inlets. The open landscape affords broad views south toward the mouth of the Sakonnet, where it empties into Rhode Island Sound.

Little Compton centers on the white frame church at one end of its traditional New England green. The green, the general store, and a neighboring restaurant are the focus of the town's day-to-day activity. At the green's opposite end a small pizzeria dispenses hot linguica grinders and other delicious sandwiches with a Portuguese touch. Little Compton, home of the Rhode Island Red, is known as the state's poultry-breeding capital.

The route continues again onto Route 77S to its end at Sakonnet Point. Stop to take in the ocean views to three sides, then return along the length of Route 77 to Tiverton.

The Basics

Start: Tiverton, located just south of Fall River, Massachusetts. From I-95 between Providence and New Bedford, Massachusetts, turn onto Rte. 24S to Tiverton. Park across from or next to the Stone Bridge Inn, on Rte. 77 a mile south of the Sakonnet Bridge, which connects Tiverton to Portsmouth.
Length: 28.5 or 13.0 miles.
Terrain: Gently rolling coastal roads.
Food: Pizza spot or general store in Little Compton at 10.8 miles. Near the end of the ride, at 20.6 miles, Tiverton Four Corners consists of little else but Gray's Ice Cream and the general store.

Miles & Directions

- 0.0 Ride south from Tiverton on Rte. 77.
- 0.7 Turn right across the short bridge, and then bear left with Nannaquaket Rd. on the other side.

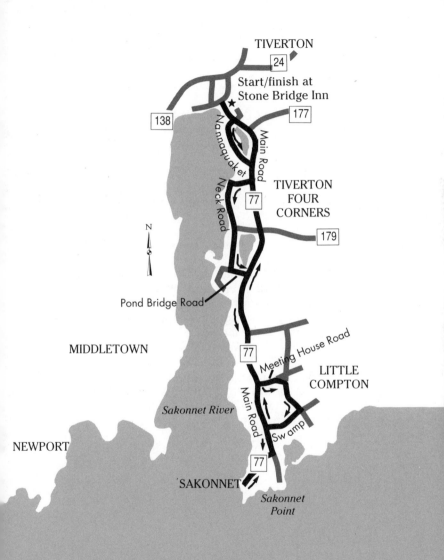

- 2.3 Merge back into Rte. 77S, keeping an eye out for the next right turn.
- 2.7 Turn right onto Seapowet Rd., which becomes Neck Rd. as it curves to the left.
- 4.1 Cross single-lane plank bridge through the wetlands of the Seapowet Wildlife Management Area.
- 6.1 Turn left onto Pond Bridge Rd. Pass dam and fish ladder at bottom of hill.
- 6.6 Turn right, again, onto Rte. 77S.

For a short, 13-mile loop, turn left here to return to Tiverton along Rte. 77N.

- 10.0 Turn left onto Meeting House Rd., following the sign toward The Comptons.
- 10.8 Arrive in Little Compton. There is a pizza place on the right, just before the town green. Other potential snack stops are the Common's Restaurant and the Wilbur General Merchandise Store across from the church on the green.
- 10.9 Turn right on the far side of the green.
- 12.0 Turn right onto Swamp Rd.
- 13.2 Turn left onto Rte. 77S to Sakonnet Point.
- 15.2 Arrive at Sakonnet Point. From here, after enjoying panoramic views of the river, the ocean, and distant Newport, simply return on Rte. 77N for the 13.3 miles back to Tiverton.
- 28.5 Arrive in Tiverton.

Vermont

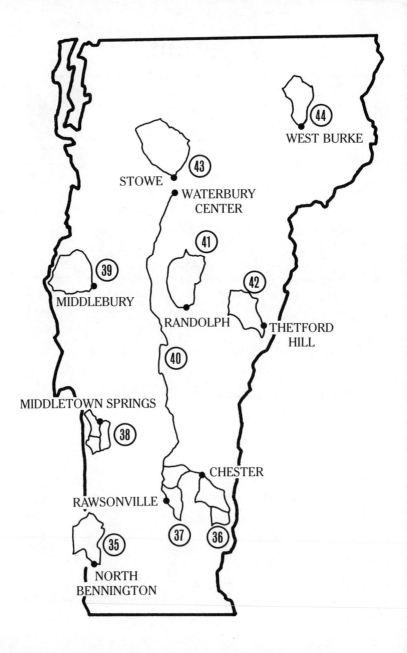

WEST BURKE 44

STOWE 43

WATERBURY
CENTER

41

42

MIDDLEBURY 39

RANDOLPH

THETFORD
HILL

40

MIDDLETOWN SPRINGS

38

CHESTER

RAWSONVILLE

37 36

35

NORTH
BENNINGTON

Vermont

Bennington to Battenkill Challenge

In the Vermont valley, the early hours of a Saturday in June belong to grazing cows and casting fly fishermen. The Bennington to Battenkill Challenge lets you in on their secret. This southwestern corner of Vermont, bounded by the Battenkill and Waloomsac rivers, hides some of the most pastoral land within three hours of Boston or four of New York.

The Challenge roughly follows the course of these two rivers as they wind their way through a landscape of rolling green hills just west of the Green Mountains. Although both flow all the way to the Hudson, the Battenkill Challenge ventures only briefly into New York before turning back into Vermont.

North Bennington, an old-time country town refreshingly free of glitz and boutiques, provides a hospitable starting point for this 41-mile tour. Park in the lot of the recently restored Victorian-style train station, which looks just as it did when built in 1890. Down the block, clustered south of the Main and Bank streets junction, Percy's Newsroom Cafe, the Main Street Cafe, and Power's Market dispense early morning breakfasts and snacks for the road.

Route 67A, the ride's initial leg, passes into open farmland in just half a mile. Also named White Creek Road, this 9-mile stretch offers a chance to warm up along a scarcely traveled road that is far preferable to the more trafficked Route 67 just to the south. On crossing into New York, the tour follows Route 22N, a busy but broad-shouldered road, for a fast 3-mile leg to Cambridge.

Running east from Cambridge, Route 313 unfolds as the highlight of the tour. Nearing the Vermont border, the road begins to run parallel to and often within sight of the Battenkill River, recognized as one of New England's best wild trout streams. Several shaded parking areas with river access allow passing cyclists to pull over and watch anglers land fighting brown, rainbow, and brook trout.

On a summer weekend you are likely to come across an inn-to-inn touring group or other cycling club along these 15 miles of road between Cambridge and Arlington. A favorite resting spot for all is the riverbank by the Bridge at the Green, a covered bridge built in 1852. It spans the Battenkill fully within sight of Route 313 halfway into the ride, a mile or two after you cross back into Vermont.

If this tour through trout-fishing country has you intrigued, consider renting a canoe from West Arlington's Battenkill Canoe Rentals for a closer look on a float downstream. Or detour north from Arlington on Route 7A for a visit to Manchester's American Museum of Fly Fishing and its neighbor, the venerable Orvis Company. Orvis has been outfitting sportfishermen since 1856. The company offers tours of its factory, where it manufactures bamboo rods, trout flies, and other fishing and outdoor equipment. Passersby are welcome as well in its retail store, which some consider the Abercrombie and Fitch of the Green Mountain State.

Arlington vies with Stockbridge, Massachusetts, for the distinction of being illustrator Norman Rockwell's home town. Both claims are just, as Rockwell lived here from 1939 to 1953, before moving south to the central Berkshire town.

The Challenge enters its toughest stretch as it turns back south from Arlington. Bypassing busy Route 7A, it enters a network of unpaved roads bordering the Green Mountain National Forest. Turning left on Maple Hill Road, gear down and prepare for a long, gradual climb along nearly 5 miles of well-maintained dirt road. Ride easily here and enjoy the intimate feel of a slow ride through a forest. You've conquered the toughest stretch once you pass the renovated Peter Matteson Tavern Museum on the left. From there, the road climbs more gently for another half mile and then becomes paved.

These back-road efforts pay off once you turn right onto Buck Hill Road, which descends almost 500 feet in 2 miles of swooping turns. Enjoy the downhill run, but don't miss some of the ride's best views along the way. Warm down along the final 2 flat miles back to North Bennington.

The Basics

Start: Park at the restored Victorian train station in North Bennington. Following Rte. 7 north through Bennington, turn west onto Rte. 67A toward Bennington College. Continue past the college into North Bennington. The station is located straight ahead on Rte. 67, here North Main St., opposite the post office.
Length: 41.3 miles.
Terrain: Rolling farmland and river valley. One gradual 2-mile climb on packed dirt road.
Food: Several parking and picnic areas along Rte. 313 on the Battenkill invite you to stop for a picnic and rest while watching fishermen cast for trout. The first of these is located at the entrance to the Battenkill Special Trout Fishing Area at 20.2 miles. The Wayside Country Store at 24.6 miles features a pleasant front stoop.

Miles and Directions

- 0.0 From the intersection of routes 67 and 67A in the center of North Bennington, ride west, passing the Merchants Bank building on your right.

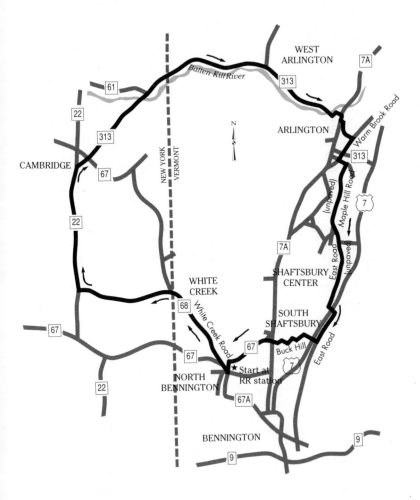

- 0.2 Right onto Rte. 38, White Creek Rd., passing the North Bennington Variety Store on your left.
- 2.9 Enter town of White Creek, marked only by a sign and a cow pasture.
- 3.8 Stay left with Rte. 38 toward Cambridge and Eagle Brook. Follow this route, ignoring all secondary turnoffs, to its intersection with Rte. 22.
- 9.1 Right onto Rte. 22N toward Cambridge. This is a fast road; ride well over to the right on the broad, paved shoulder.
- 12.6 Right onto Rte. 313E, here named Gilbert St., toward Arlington, over 15 miles distant on this road. Downtown Cambridge is straight ahead.
- 17.6 Continue straight as a road to the left detours to the Eagleville covered bridge. You may detour as well, if you wish, for a first glimpse of the Battenkill.
- 20.2 Parking area with river access on right. Route enters Battenkill Special Trout Fishing Area.
- 21.0 Sprint for Vermont state line; halfway point of the ride.
- 24.6 Pass Wayside Country Store, a potential snack stop, on the right.
- 27.1 Enter West Arlington. Battenkill Canoe Rentals on the right.
- 27.9 Turn right onto Rte.7A toward Bennington.
- 28.0 Left onto East Arlington Rd., opposite Country Variety Store.
- 28.6 Right on Warm Brook Rd.
- 29.6 Left on Maple Hill Rd., which soon becomes a well-maintained dirt road. In a quarter mile, follow it to the right as a poorly maintained dirt road continues straight.
- 32.6 At the fork, bear left onto East Rd., which is still unpaved. Maple Hill Rd. continues straight, then turns to the right toward Rte. 7A. The next mile presents this ride's most demanding hill, a steady grade up a rough surface. The road becomes paved again, at the end of a long climb, a half mile beyond the Peter Matteson Tavern Museum on the left.
- 37.2 Right on Buck Hill Rd., the first paved road to the right. Following a short climb, Buck Hill Rd. descends almost 500

feet in 2 miles of swooping turns. Buck Hill Rd. becomes East Rd. again toward the bottom.

- 39.1 Continue straight through flashing red light, across Rte. 7A and onto Church St. in South Shaftsbury.
- 39.5 Bear left onto Rte. 67 at stop sign, immediately after crossing railroad tracks. Ride with caution, as this is a blind curve for traffic coming from the right.
- 41.1 Follow Rte. 67 as it turns left, becoming North Main St., into North Bennington.
- 41.3 Return to train station on the left.

36

Chester Country Weekend: Saxtons River Cruise

*Chester—Grafton—Cambridgeport
Saxtons River—Westminster—Saxtons River
Bartonsville—Chester*

Bob Maynard, president of the Vermont Country Cyclers inn-to-inn touring company, recommends the southeastern corner of Vermont as offering some of the finest cycling in New England. The Chester Country Weekend explores this countryside of hills, river valleys, and perfect Vermont villages. This has ranked among VCC's most popular outings since Maynard founded the company in 1979.

The Chester Country Weekend features two days of riding that start and end in Chester. The first day's Saxtons River Cruise, 46 or 25 miles long, rolls southeast toward the Connecticut River. The second day's West River Challenge loops for 52 or 30 miles southwest to the boundary of the Green Mountain National Forest.

Whether you choose the longer or the shorter options or plan to spend only one day on the bike, combine your rides with a country inn stay for a perfect weekend of R&R and exercise. Vermont Country Cyclers puts its riders up at the Stone Hearth Inn, 2 miles from downtown Chester. This former farmhouse is also a member of Cycle Inn Vermont, an affiliation of five inns that transport baggage and otherwise cater to guests biking between them. (The others are located to the north, in Gassetts and Ludlow.) Chester Inn, larger and less intimate than the Stone Hearth, has an outdoor swimming pool, tennis courts, and a sauna to complement the back-roads cycling just outside its front door. The Chester Chamber of Commerce operates an information booth in the center of town and can also help you find accommodations, especially if you call ahead.

The initial stretch of the Saxtons River Cruise follows an old stagecoach route over hilly terrain, ending with a beautiful descent into the classic New England town of Grafton. This town was home to 10,000 sheep and several woolen mills before the Civil War, after which it fell on hard times. In the past several decades, the private Windham Foundation has spurred the town's revival as a tourism center. These efforts have clearly paid off. The Grafton Village Apple Company and the Grafton Village Cheese Company are worth detours for those interested in seeing the sights and getting fed too.

From Grafton the route follows the Saxtons River to the town of the same name. The shorter option turns north from here, directly back to Chester. The longer option continues south over rolling terrain toward Westminster, a calm village located on the mile-wide plain of one of the Connecticut River valley's terrace formations. This 46-miler then returns to Saxtons River and follows the same route as the 25-mile ride back to Chester. Both rides cross many short hills. The longer option adds a gradual 3-miler as well.

If you're a covered bridge fan—and what better excuse for a rest is there—look for the recently rebuilt Saxtons River bridge on the right just a mile before you return to Saxtons River. The reconstruction used the same building techniques originally employed back in 1867. Two more covered bridges follow, both spanning the Williams River off Route 103 in Bartonsville. You will have to detour about a half mile to see either of these.

If you arrive back in Chester with an unplanned afternoon still ahead, consider calling Vermont Village Walks, which is head-quartered in Chester. Their guides can provide maps for, lead you along, or simply point you toward several short local trails. There's nothing like a bike and hike weekend to work up an appetite and ensure a good night's sleep.

The Basics

Start: Chester. Located 8 miles southeast of Springfield, Chester is most easily reached from exit 6 off I-91. Follow Rte. 103 west for 10 miles into town. Route distances are measured from Chester's main intersection, where routes 103, 11, and 35 converge.

Length: 46.4 or 25.4 miles.

Terrain: Hilly, with one 3-mile climb on the longer option.

Food: Grafton Village Store and Grafton Village Apple Company in Grafton at 7.2 miles. Tiffany's Bakery and Pizza, Paul and Mary in Saxtons River at 14.1 miles (and again at 34.6 miles on the longer option).

Miles and Directions

- 0.0 From Chester ride south on Rte. 35, a rolling road with some steep climbs, toward Grafton.
- 7.0 Left onto Rte. 121E, following the Saxtons River downstream toward the Connecticut River.

To visit Grafton, with its Village Store and Apple Company, detour right onto Rte. 121W. The store is only 0.2 miles distant. The Apple Company is another 1.5 miles down Rte. 121W, which becomes dirt here. For an additional excursion, turn left after the Village Store at the sign for Brattleboro and Stratton, passing the Old Tavern on your right as

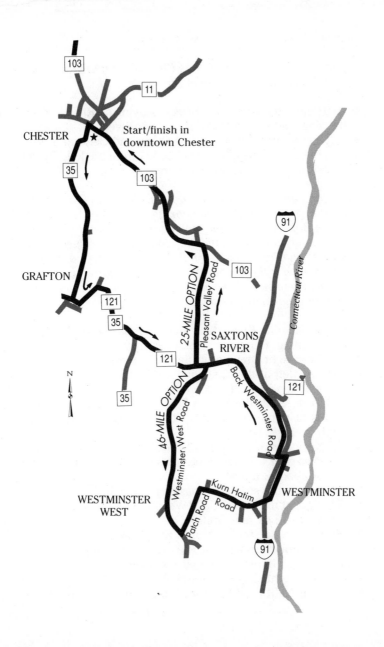

*you turn. The Grafton Village Cheese Company and a cov-
ered bridge lie 1 mile down the road.*

- 10.9 Bear left crossing the bridge, staying on Rte. 121E. Follow the sign toward the town of Saxtons River.
- 11.1 Pass Cambridgeport Post Office and General Store.
- 13.8 Pleasant Valley Rd. joins Rte.121 from the left. The longer and shorter options diverge here.

*To complete the 25.4-mile ride, turn left onto Pleasant Val-
ley Rd., going uphill. Then bear right after the Mustard Seed
Home Bakery on the left, staying on Pleasant Valley Rd. At
21.3 miles, turn left onto Rte. 103N, which returns you to
downtown Chester at 25.4 miles. For the longer option, this
intersection is the knot at the center of a figure-eight circuit;
you will return on Pleasant Valley Rd. after completing the
loop through Westminster.*

- 14.1 In Saxtons River, turn right across the bridge with the green railing, following signs to Putney.
- 14.4 Bear right, staying on the main road.
- 20.0 Bear left at the Y, staying on the paved road. The Maple Grove Schoolhouse is up on the right.
- 21.2 Turn left at the Y onto Patch Rd. just before the bridge. This is also known as Kurn Hatim Rd. Begin 3-mile gradual climb.
- 26.7 Kurn Hatim Children's School on the left.
- 27.0 Pass over I-91 and continue straight. I-91 will be on your left for about 2 miles.
- 29.0 Left at the stop sign, passing under I-91.
- 29.5 Right at the T onto Back Westminster Rd., following signs to Saxtons River and Grafton.
- 32.3 Left at the stop sign onto Rte. 121W.
- 34.6 Continue straight on Rte. 121 across the green bridge and through the town of Saxtons River.
- 35.1 Bear right, staying on Rte. 121W.
- 35.4 Bear right onto Pleasant Valley Rd. going uphill.

- 35.7 Bear right, staying on Pleasant Valley Rd., after passing the Mustard Seed Home Bakery on the left.
- 40.3 Left at stop sign onto Rte. 103N, which follows Williams River into Chester for the next 6 miles.
- 44.2 Chester General Store on the left.
- 46.4 Return to intersection with routes 11 and 35 in Chester.

37

Chester Country Weekend: West River Challenge

Chester—Weston—Londonderry
Rawsonville—Jamaica—West Townshend
South Windham—North Windham—Chester

The Chester Country Weekend's second day explores the eastern foothills of the Green Mountains. A 30-mile and a 52-mile loop each cross from Chester to the West River's valley, where restored villages cluster in the shadows of forested mountain walls. Both rides feature challenging but rewarding climbs that pass through hilltop settlements definitely off the beaten track.

The West River Challenge reaches its first stop in Weston, situated at the north end of the West River Valley. Lay your bikes down and rest by the bandstand on the oval green, which was a shallow frog pond before the Civil War. Visit the columned Weston Playhouse, the oldest continuously operated summer theater in Vermont.

The longer and shorter rides diverge in Londonderry. The shorter option turns back toward Chester from this ski lodge town, climbing out of the valley for 2 miles to the base of the Magic Mountain Ski Area. The longer option loops south, and then the two rejoin at North Windham.

The 52-mile route adds both distance and a difficult climb. First, a 2-mile roller-coaster uphill along combined routes 30 and 100 passes the access road to Ball Mountain Lake. Controlled releases from the dam across the West River here create an excellent stretch of white water downstream for an annual canoe race. Jamaica State Park, off Route 100 on the other side of Ball Mountain, has a swimming and picnic area. Local legend has it that in 1799 the first minister of the white congregational church of the town of Jamaica was dismissed for selling his wife to another man. She, this antique rumor adds, was pleased with the transaction.

The loop turns north from West Townshend, which is located on the plain above a wide oxbow bend in the river, and follows a back road that climbs steeply for almost 3 miles along Turkey Mountain Brook. At the end of the climb is Windham, at 2,000 feet the second-highest village in Vermont.

Both routes pass through Simonsville, a small village strung along the banks of a pebbly mountain stream, on the return leg to Chester. Rowells Inn, built by Simons himself in 1820, has served generations of travelers. First it was a stagecoach stop on this road over the hills. In the early automobile days, it was an overnight stop on the scenic tour from the White Mountains of New Hampshire to Manchester in the heart of the Green Mountains.

From Simonsville, the West River Challenge continues along this upland river valley, crossing and recrossing the rocky Williams River on its way back to Chester.

The Basics

Start: Chester. Located 8 miles southeast of Springfield, Chester is most easily reached from exit 6 off I-91. Follow Rte. 103 west for 10 miles into town.
Length: 52.5 or 30.3 miles.
Terrain: Hilly.
Food: Several options, plus a swimming hole, in Jamaica at 29.5 miles.

Miles & Directions

- 0.0 From downtown Chester, at the intersection of routes 11, 103, and 35, ride west on Rte. 11 toward Weston and Londonderry.
- 2.1 Pass the Motel in the Meadow on the right.
- 4.4 Right onto paved road, following sign to Weston and Andover. Chesterfield's Restaurant is on the right as you turn.
- 5.2 Bear left at the Y, staying on the main road.
- 6.7 Continue straight through Andover.
- 7.4 Bear left at the Y. You don't have to climb East Hill.
- 7.8 Horse Shoe Acres marks the beginning of a 3-mile climb that gets steep in spots.
- 10.6 Top of hill!
- 11.6 Fresh springwater on the left.
- 12.2 Left at the stop sign onto Rte. 100S.
- 12.4 Pass through Weston; its oval common and bandstand make for a nice initial rest stop. Continue on Rte. 100S toward Londonderry.
- 12.7 The Weston House on the left marks the beginning of a gradual 2-mile climb.
- 17.7 Turn left in Londonderry onto Rte. 11E, riding across the bridge ahead. Then immediately . . .
- 17.8 Turn right onto Middletown Rd. and begin a mile-long climb.

The shorter, 30.3-mile ride diverges here by continuing straight on Rte. 11E to Chester. A 2-mile climb beginning at the entrance to the Magic Mountain Ski Area is the only major obstacle remaining. From the junction with Rte. 121, continue on Rte. 11E downstream alongside the Middle Branch of the Williams River for the final 8 miles to Chester.

- 19.3 As you continue up Middletown Rd. on the longer ride, a cemetery on your right marks the top of the climb. Use caution descending from here. It gets very steep just before an upcoming stop sign.

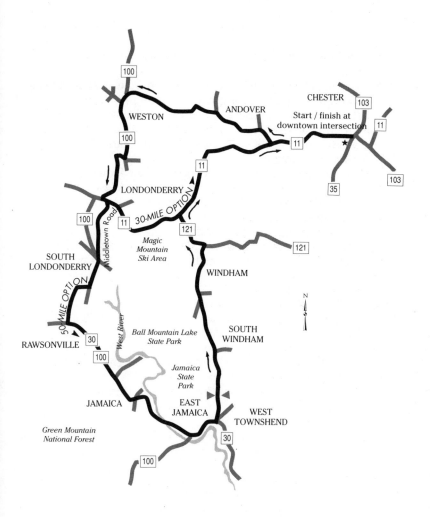

100

WESTON

ANDOVER

CHESTER

103

Start / finish at
downtown intersection

11

100

11

100

LONDONDERRY

30-MILE OPTION

11

11

121

35

103

Magic
Mountain
Ski Area

121

121

SOUTH
LONDONDERRY

Middletown Road

WINDHAM

50-MILE OPTION

West River

Ball Mountain Lake
State Park

SOUTH
WINDHAM

RAWSONVILLE

30

100

Jamaica
State
Park

N

JAMAICA

EAST
JAMAICA

WEST
TOWNSHEND

Green Mountain
National Forest

30

100

- 20.5 Continue straight at the stop sign onto Rte. 100S.
- 24.6 Left at the stop sign onto combined routes 30 and 100S, following the signs to Jamaica. Begin 2-mile roller-coaster climb.
- 27.0 Ride with caution on the following 2-mile descent into Jamaica.
- 29.5 Cross bridge into Jamaica and continue straight through town. For a detour to a great swimming hole, turn left just before the bridge. You will see the pool down the embankment to your right. You could turn this into a lunch stop with a sandwich from BK's Grocery Store, the Jamaica House, or the Bavaria House.
- 32.5 Continue straight on Rte. 30S in East Jamaica.
- 33.5 Left onto paved but unmarked road in West Townshend. The 1848 Country Store is opposite the turn on the right. Begin steep 3-mile climb.
- 36.5 Pass through South Windham.
- 38.4 Pavement ends. Always ride slowly on dirt roads!
- 39.1 Continue straight through staggered four-way intersection.
- 40.0 Pavement begins.
- 41.4 Dirt road again, but for less than a half mile.
- 42.2 Left at four-way intersection onto Rte. 121W (although this is probably not marked), and begin a short climb.
- 44.2 Right at the stop sign onto Rte. 11E, which follows the Middle Branch of the Williams River all the way back to Chester.
- 50.5 Return to intersection in downtown Chester.

38

Middletown Springs Triple Option Cruise

Middletown Springs
Poultney—Wells—Pawlet
Danby Four Corners
Tinmouth—Middletown Springs

This triple option ride, recommended by Vermont Country Cyclers, gives you a choice of loops of 26, 35, or 41 miles. All feature excellent picnicking and swimming along the rocky banks of the Poultney River and the sandy shores of Lake St. Catherine. The area's quiet roads lead through an intimate landscape of orchards, farms, summer homes, and small villages. Middletown Springs itself was established in the nineteenth century as a health spa. The town featured supposedly restorative iron and sulphur springs, where Victorian-era men and women could go and "take the cure."

The first town west from Middletown Springs is East Poultney, where Ethan Allen and the Green Mountain Boys frequented the Eagle Tavern in the 1790s. Perhaps they were still celebrating their capture of Fort Ticonderoga from the British at the outset of the American Revolution. One story relates that during this post-Revolutionary period a Captain William Watson raised his glass in this toast: "The enemies of our country! May they have cobweb breeches, a porcupine saddle, a hard-trotting horse, and an eternal journey." May the remainder of this ride prove free of such a curse.

Route 30 runs close above the broken shoreline of Lake St. Catherine, which stretches southward among low hills. New York's Taconic Range is visible across the water. The slate ledges of St. Catherine Mountain press in on the left. Just beyond, an access road crosses the lake's southern neck, giving you the option of exploring its opposite shore.

You do not have to decide which route to follow until you reach the town of Wells, at Lake St. Catherine's end. Here, a back road turns east, crossing the hill back to Middletown Springs along a partially dirt road.

Both longer rides continue to the town of Pawlet, which is crowded haphazardly into a narrow valley where Flower Brook and the Mettawee River join. Visit Mach's General Store (where you can look through the grate in the back to the river below), the Pawlet Potter, and the Station Restaurant. Beyond Pawlet, the middle-distance option turns north for the final 10 miles back to Middletown Springs.

The 41-mile ride climbs for 2 miles to the mountain settlement of Danby Four Corners, situated on a plateau of farmland, then turns north through the smaller upland village of Tinmouth. Tinmouth was an iron and forge town in the early part of the nineteenth century. Dairy farming, however, evolved as the leading industry over the next hundred years. In the last few decades, as Vermont agriculture in general has declined, many old pastures here have grown over. The town is now dotted with remaining farms and summer homes.

The Basics

Start: Middletown Springs, just southeast of Rutland. You can reach Middletown Springs by following Rte. 140 west for 9 miles from Rte. 7. Ride distances are measured from the Middletown Springs Inn, on the right just before Rte. 133 turns left.
Length: 26.5, 34.7, or 40.7 miles.

Terrain: The longer ride tackles two steep hills leading to Danby Four Corners. Otherwise, all three options feature rolling hills with only moderate climbs.

Food: Each of the five towns along the way has its general store. Pawlet, at 23.1 miles, offers the most options—a general store, an ice cream shop, and a restaurant. Those on the shortest option can snack on the town green in Wells.

Miles & Directions

- 0.0 Turn right from Middletown Springs Inn onto Rte. 140W.
- 0.1 Continue straight at the stop sign, staying on Rte. 140W for the next 8 miles.
- 6.8 Pass through East Poultney; a general store and town green are on the left.
- 8.3 Left at stoplight, following signs for Rte. 30S. To visit Green Mountain College and The Original Vermont Store, continue straight on Rte. 140W into Poultney.
- 8.4 Left at blinking red light, following signs for Rte. 30S and Lake St. Catherine.
- 8.7 Bear right, crossing the Poultney River. Stay on Rte. 30S for the next 8 miles.
- 11.5 Lake St. Catherine State Park. Swimming, picnic area, bathrooms, and refreshments on the right.
- 14.2 Access road to West Shore. Check it out if you wish, but return to Rte. 30S.
- 16.7 Enter village of Wells, The two longer rides bear right here, then immediately turn left onto Wells Rd. just past Nancy's General Store.

The shorter, 26.5-mile option turns left onto Tinmouth Rd., past Nancy's General Store on the right and the town green on the left. Tinmouth Rd. will soon begin a 3-mile climb, with a mile-long unpaved section. Turn left at the stop sign at 21.4 miles, onto Rte. 133N. It's mostly downhill from here back to the intersection with Rte. 140 in Middletown Springs.

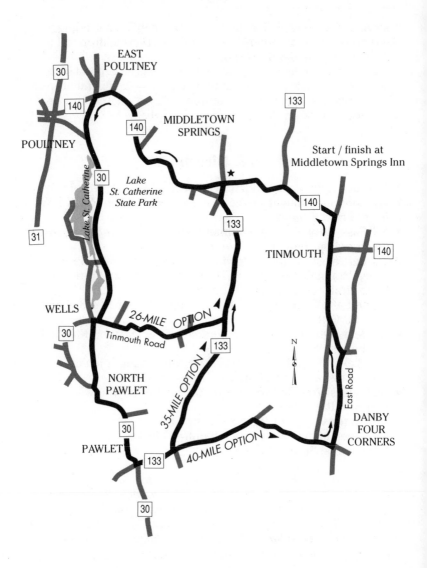

30

EAST
POULTNEY

140

MIDDLETOWN
SPRINGS

133

140

POULTNEY

140

Start / finish at
Middletown Springs Inn

30

Lake
St. Catherine
State Park

140

Lake St. Catherine

31

133

140

TINMOUTH

133

WELLS

26-MILE OPTION

30

Tinmouth Road

133

N

NORTH
PAWLET

35-MILE OPTION

East Road

DANBY
FOUR
CORNERS

30

PAWLET

133

40-MILE OPTION

30

- 19.7 Left at the stop sign back onto Rte. 30S, cresting the hill to your left.
- 23.1 Left onto Rte. 133 in Pawlet. As noted above, this is a fine spot to stop for lunch.
- 24.4 Continue straight if riding the longer, 40.7-mile ride.

The shorter, 34.7-mile ride bears left with Rte. 133N, which climbs gradually for 5 miles and then descends for another 5 all the way back to the intersection with Rte. 140 in Middletown Springs. The longer option continues straight, passing a yellow house and large red barn on the left.

- 25.5 Begin steep 2-mile climb.
- 27.5 Red barn on the right marks the top.
- 29.0 Left at stop sign in Danby Four Corners. General Store on the right. You will be on East Rd. now for 3 miles.
- 32.0 Left onto paved side road marked "TH2" (watch closely). A small white house will be on your right after you turn. Be careful not to continue straight toward Danby.
- 35.4 In Tinmouth continue straight onto Rte. 140W at the fire station. Stay on Rte. 140 for the next 3 miles. Sharp turns and hills ahead.
- 38.7 Left at stop sign onto combined routes 140W and 133S, following sign to Middletown Springs.
- 40.7 Arrive back at Middletown Springs Inn, just before intersection where Rte. 133 turns left.

39

Champlain Valley Cruise

Middlebury—Chimney Point—Vergennes
Weybridge—Middlebury

Out-of-staters normally think of Vermont as a land of green mountains and hills with hardly a stretch of level cycling around. But cycling in Vermont does not necessarily mean pedaling toward the clouds. The Champlain Valley Cruise, nominated as one of New England's finest rides by several of the Vermont Bicycle Touring company's leaders, proves this point. The tour rolls over a mild series of north-south ridges from Middlebury to the shores of Lake Champlain, passing cow pastures, cranberry bogs, and a waterfowl preserve along the way. In May the green fields sparkle with dandelion blossoms. In October the skies sound with ducks and geese winging south.

The ride next turns north along the shores of Lake Champlain, the sixth-largest body of fresh water in the United States. Long and slender, the lake stretches for 110 miles along the border between Vermont and New York. Its shoreline is largely undeveloped, and nearly one hundred mostly uninhabited islands dot its surface. The town square in Vergennes, the self-proclaimed "smallest city in America," offers a resting point two-thirds of the way along the loop. From there, the ride follows Otter Creek, the state's longest river, back to Middlebury.

One and one-half miles out of Middlebury, stop to visit the Morgan Horse Farm in Weybridge. The farm is owned and operated by the University of Vermont. Visitors may tour the large barn where the descendants of the original Justin Morgan horse are bred, trained, and housed.

Although this tour is more than 40 miles long, beginning-to-intermediate cyclists should have no trouble completing it. Just go slow, enjoy the views, and stop to rest at the high points along the way.

The Basics

Start: Middlebury, in west-central Vermont. Park near the town green, at the intersection of routes 7 and 125.
Length: 43.9 miles.
Terrain: Mostly flat to Vergennes. Mildly rolling hills from Vergennes to Middlebury.
Food: The Family Restaurant at the intersection of routes 125 and 17 at 16.4 miles offers lunch, either inside or on picnic tables. There are a general store and a water fountain at the Vergennes town green at 30.4 miles.

Miles & Directions

- 0.0 Head west on Rte. 125 out of Middlebury, passing the Middlebury College campus at the edge of town.
- 8.7 Right at T onto Rte. 22A-N.
- 9.0 Almost immediate left, at Pratt's Gulf station, back onto Rte. 125W.
- 15.6 Reach Lake Champlain and see Chimney Point bridge ahead.
- 16.4 At the Family Restaurant, turn right on Rte. 17W toward DAR State Park.
- 18.4 Bear left onto Lake St. at Jean's Country Store. An easy turn to miss, this is the first left after you pass the DAR Strong House a half mile back.
- 25.5 Lake St. turns right, becoming Pease Rd. Do not continue straight onto gravel road.

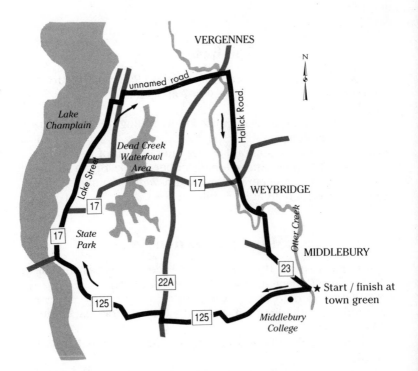

- 26.0 Left at T onto unnamed road.
- 26.4 Turn right on second unnamed road, toward Vergennes.
- 30.2 "Welcome to Vergennes—The Smallest City in the U.S.A."
- 30.4 Left onto Rte. 22A, Main St.; cross Otter Creek and climb two steep blocks to the town square. There is a water fountain here for bottle refills.
- 30.8 Right on Maple St. at the corner of the town square nearest the bridge. Leaving Vergennes, see Snake Mountain ahead and to the right.
- 36.9 Cross Rte. 17, continuing straight on what is now Hallick Rd.
- 38.9 Enter Weybridge, crossing Otter Creek as it pours through a turbine dam on its way to Lake Champlain. Turn right coming across the bridge.
- 40.9 Bear left onto Rte. 23 at Weybridge Hill, with cemetery on right.
- 43.9 Arrive in Middlebury. Rte. 23 ends at T with Rte. 125.

40

Tour of Scenic Rural Vermont Classic

Rawsonville—Londonderry—Ludlow
Sherburne Center—Stockbridge—Granville
Warren—Waitsfield—Waterbury Center
and back

More than 200 miles—in two days? After sleeping in a barn? You call that fun? You bet! It's also called the Tour of Scenic Rural Vermont, a back-to-back century ride through the heartland of the Green Mountain State.

An annual tour of this route, called TOSRV–East, is sponsored by the Greater Boston Council of American Youth Hostels. Al Lester, the organization's president and touring director, has earned his status as one of New England's premier bike tour organizers. Two of his annual American Youth Hostel tours, the Tour of Scenic Rural Vermont and the Cape in a Day ride, have won mythic reputations in the regional cycling scene. Both are included in this selection of New England's best rides. They are for serious cyclists only.

This Vermont tradition started in 1972, when three cycling friends decided to organize a tour modeled after the then ten-year-old Tour of the Scioto River Valley in Ohio. This original TOSRV, which draws thousands of participants annually, has since spawned at least twenty-five other cross-state rides. A series of twelve such rides from Washington State to Maine are now scheduled consecutively to facilitate transcontinental rides. For more information about this cross-country marathon, contact the Annual Fit-Fest Bike Ride Across America (AFF-BRAAM) in Northfield, Minnesota 55057.

The sheer length of this Vermont ride is not as important as its heroic nature. Many cyclists make Vermont's TOSRV the centerpiece of every season. One veteran has completed it in each of its seventeen years. Certain stretches of the route have legends associated with them. Riders talk of the opening climb to Terrible Mountain and descent to the shore of Lake Rescue. Omens of the weekend ahead? A competition develops to do "the Wall" in a racing freewheel. Then, after the final short climbs over the Duxbury Hills, the reward—a visit to Ben & Jerry's ice cream factory in Waterbury.

Your companions range from the deadly serious to the eccentric. One rider rode to Rawsonville from Falmouth, Massachusetts, completed the tour, and rode home again. Another rode fueled by a long day's worth of bananas taped to his frame tubes. One couple powering a tandem bike covered the 204 miles in a single day.

Most, however, are just active bikers, a mix of those who keep coming back every year and those who join for the first time. They ride alone, with a friend, or in groups. Ages range from fifteen to old enough that they won't tell you. Their paces range from 10 miles per hour to 20, including rest stops.

They take off at 7:00 A.M. from The Rafters, a rustic overnight shelter just south of Rawsonville. Highlights en route include pedaling past the Okemo, Killington, Sugarbush, and Mad River Glen ski areas; the view to Moss Glen Falls from Granville Notch; and countless lakes, brooks, farms, and mountain vistas. The day ends with a carbohydrate-loaded feast and overnight stay at Waterbury center's Ski Hostel Lodge. After a Sunday morning breakfast, they're off again, slower and with a southerly view.

Participation in this AYH tour, which includes official checkpoints and sag wagon service, is limited to eighty per year. Places are usually filled way in advance. Write the Greater Boston Council of the American Youth Hostels (1020 Common-wealth Avenue, Boston, MA 02215) for more information.

Or you can organize your own group. Make sure you reserve accommodations at both ends in advance and train adequately beforehand. Route 100 is a very busy though scenic north-south route, not a back road, so ride with caution and with respect for everybody else on the road.

If you conquer the Cape in a Day (or Two) Classic and the Tour of Scenic Rural Vermont and still want to up your mileage, Call Al Lester and ask him about his ultraride, the Tour of New England. Jointly sponsored by AYH and the Charles River Wheelmen, this three-day marathon touches all six New England states in 350 hilly miles.

The Basics

Start: This overnight tour starts in Rawsonville, 7 miles south of Londonderry on Route 100.
Length: 102 miles per day for two days; 204 miles total.
Terrain: Hilly, with three major climbs.
Food: Numerous snack and lunch stops along the way. Riders normally stop for rest and fuel at Jim & Zel's in Bridgewater at 38.3 miles, at the Stockbridge General Store in Stockbridge at 53.9 miles, and at the Phyl-Den Dairy Barn in Waitsfield at 85.9 miles.

Miles & Directions

■ 0.0 From the intersection of Rte. 100 and Rte. 30 in Rawsonville, head north on Rte. 100 toward South Londonderry and Londonderry. The directions from here are simple: Continue on Rte. 100N for the next 102 miles to Waterbury Center. Retrace your ride back to Rawsonville on the second day. Mileage to each town, noted going northward, is presented below.

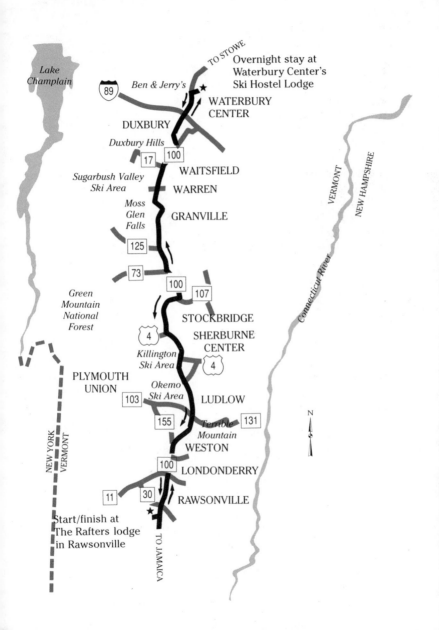

Lake
Champlain

89

TO STOWE

Ben & Jerry's

Overnight stay at
Waterbury Center's
Ski Hostel Lodge

WATERBURY
CENTER

DUXBURY

Duxbury Hills

17   100

WAITSFIELD

Sugarbush Valley
Ski Area

WARREN

Moss
Glen
Falls

GRANVILLE

125

73

100   107

STOCKBRIDGE

Green
Mountain
National
Forest

4

SHERBURNE
CENTER

Killington
Ski Area

4

PLYMOUTH
UNION

Okemo
Ski Area

LUDLOW

103

155

Terrible
Mountain

131

WESTON

100   LONDONDERRY

11   30

RAWSONVILLE

NEW YORK
VERMONT

Start/finish at
The Rafters lodge
in Rawsonville

TO JAMAICA

VERMONT
NEW HAMPSHIRE

Connecticut River

N

- 4.0 South Londonderry
- 7.0 Londonderry
- 12.0 Weston
- 23.0 Ludlow
- 32.0 Plymouth Union
- 41.0 Sherburne Center
- 51.0 Pittsfield
- 54.0 Stockbridge
- 62.0 Rochester
- 70.0 Granville
- 81.0 Warren
- 87.0 Waitsfield
- 98.0 Duxbury
- 102.0 Waterbury Center

Randolph Challenge

Randolph—Roxbury—Northfield Center
Williamstown—Brookfield
Randolph Center—Randolph

The Vermont Bicycle Touring company hails the Randolph Challenge as a favorite of its particularly fit and fearless guests. This 49-mile tour includes two long climbs that occasional riders may wish to avoid. Those eager to accept the challenge will reap the rewards of a tour through heartland Vermont, past farmland and forest that still appears much as it did generations ago.

Randolph, the tour's starting point, lies at the head of the White River, three of whose branches fork northward, carving out the ridges and valleys this ride follows. Randolph is an old railroad town known as the home of the first pure breed of American horses. It was here, in 1795, that Justin Morgan brought the two-year-old colt that founded the Morgan breed. Today Randolph is home to several country inns, Vermont Castings (a premier manufacturer of wood-burning stoves), and a range of local businesses.

Once pedaling north on Route 12A, start enjoying the scenery and don't worry about directions for a while. The next turn, in Northfield, is over 20 miles distant. Halfway along, Route 12A begins to climb gradually as its river valley narrows. Rice, Adams, and Lost mountains press in on the left. Roxbury State Forest borders the road on the right. A fifty-year-old guide to the

Green Mountain State notes that "this is one of the last regions in the state where bear can still be found." Look out, in case any have survived the last half century here in the hills.

The small village of Roxbury, located at the head of the valley, signals the climb's end. From here the road begins to descend, following the path of the Dog River toward Northfield Center. A new valley opens in its path.

For cyclists exploring central Vermont, the law of the mountains dictates that while north-south roads roll more or less flat, those crossing from east to west must traverse the ridges separating one long valley from another. The Randolph Challenge proves the law's truth after 22 miles of relatively easy riding. Turning east, Route 64 climbs for almost 4 miles before finally plunging through hillsides of farmland toward Williamstown.

Four miles south of Williamstown, Route 14 enters Ainsworth State Park and twists through the Williamstown Gulf, where the valley's walls converge to form a deep, narrow pass. This is an ideal resting spot on a hot day. The sun scarcely penetrates this cut, and the fern-covered banks of a roadside stream are a nice place to stretch out before you tackle the second big climb.

South of Ainsworth State Park, a 5-mile-long ascent to the town of Brookfield and beyond occurs in a dozen steps along two roads. The monotony of the first stretch toward Brookfield makes the climb seem tougher than it really is. Then the route turns south, and an unnamed road toward Randolph climbs the crest of an open ridge facing the Green Mountains to the right and the White Mountains to the left. This second leg offers views that will soon make you forget how long it's been since you rode level ground.

For a rest on the way up this ridge, detour into the four-corners village of Brookfield. To reach Brookfield, simply continue straight on Route 65 past the left turn back toward Randolph. Once in the village you can have a swim and a look at the community's top tourist attraction: the Brookfield Floating Bridge. First built in 1820 of 380 tarred and lashed barrels, the Floating Bridge is the only one of its kind in Vermont and one of only two in the entire country. Thirteen mills once lined

Sunset Lake, also known as Mirror Lake or Colts Pond. Also stop by the Newton House, built in 1832 and now maintained as a museum, although it is open only on July and August Sunday afternoons. Organized bike tours frequent the Green Trails Inn, which doubles as a ski-touring center in the winter.

The Basics

Start: Randolph. Take exit 4 off I-89 and follow Route 66 West for 3 miles. There is public parking behind the Adult Basic Education Center, on the right in the center of town.
Length: 49.0 miles.
Terrain: Two climbs, each over 2 miles long. Otherwise moderate—for Vermont.
Food: Pack your own. There are several picnic spots but no stores until the very end.

Miles & Directions

- 0.0 Leaving the parking lot in Randolph, turn right onto Rte. 66E.
- 0.2 Right onto Rte. 12A at intersection of routes 66, 12, and 12A. Continue on 12A for 20.9 miles toward Northfield.
- 14.0 Continue straight through village of Roxbury.
- 18.8 Sprint for the Northfield town line.
- 21.1 Right on Rte. 12S.
- 22.2 Left at bottom of short hill onto Rte. 64E toward Williamstown and I-89.
- 26.0 Climb ends shortly after you pass beneath I-89 overpass. Rte. 12 begins sweeping downhill run into Williamstown.
- 29.0 Entering Williamstown, right onto Rte. 14S toward Brookfield.
- 33.0 Pass through the thick woods of Ainsworth State Park.
- 36.6 Right onto Rte. 65, which climbs in several large steps

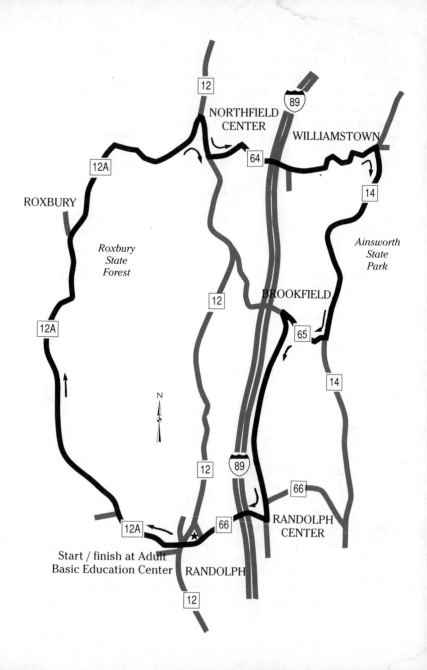

12

NORTHFIELD
CENTER

89

WILLIAMSTOWN

12A

64

ROXBURY

14

*Roxbury
State
Forest*

*Ainsworth
State
Park*

12

BROOKFIELD

12A

65

14

N

12

12

89

66

12A

66

RANDOLPH
CENTER

Start / finish at Adult
Basic Education Center   RANDOLPH

12

toward Brookfield. Signs may point toward Floating Bridge, a Brookfield attraction.

- 38.9 Left onto unnamed road at top of climb immediately after you pass a church on the left. This is the first paved road to the left on Rte. 65. (Or detour straight for a visit to Brookfield.)
- 45.0 Merge right onto Rte. 66W toward Randolph.
- 45.7 Wills General Store on left.
- 46.0 Stay right with Rte. 66 for the final 3-mile downhill into Randolph.
- 49.0 Arrive back in Randolph town center.

42

Orange County Challenge

Thetford—Post Mills—West Fairlee
Vershire—Chelsea
Tunbridge—South Strafford—Thetford

The Orange County Challenge explores an untouristed Vermont of wooded valleys, hilltop farms, and lush pastureland. The tour neighbors the preceding Randolph Challenge and explores similar river and ridge terrain.

Each of the roads along this route, as with most in the hill countries of Vermont and New Hampshire, follows the path of a river or stream. The roads are steepest when they cross a watershed from one trickle to another. The Orange County Challenge features two such ascents, although the first begins easily as a barely perceptible incline along peaceful Route 113 toward Chelsea.

This road follows the nearly unpronounceable Ompompanoosuc River to its source, a string of bubbling springs near the crest of Judgement Ridge. Located halfway along this climb, the small village of Vershire shows little evidence of once having supported a population of more than 2,000. This was the country's leading copper-mining center a century ago but seems to have attracted no industry since. From Judgement Ridge, Route 113 follows the steep downhill course of Jail Brook to the town of Cheshire. Here, 20 miles into the ride, two country stores and a village green provide welcome opportunities to stop and stretch.

As you ride from Chelsea toward Tunbridge, it is difficult to visualize the pioneer days when this pleasant valley was a favorite warpath for raiding Indians. Today these 8 miles of roadway are lined on the right side with summer cottages and gentlemen's farms and bordered on the left by the southward-flowing First Branch of the White River.

The climb from Tunbridge toward Strafford crosses this route's second watershed. A narrow, unnamed road winds up a hillside whose meadows are dotted with wildflowers throughout the spring, summer, and fall. This is a steep climb, and your group may want to split up so that each rider can ride at his or her own pace to the top. Regroup at the climb's end, where a lone roadside oak tree provides shade from the sun or protection against the light rains that often enshroud these hilltops. After a short rest, you may coast for the next 8 downhill miles, braking only for a few sharp turns and short sections of well-graded dirt road. A monument to Justin Morrill Smith, who represented Vermont in the U.S. House of Representatives and Senate in the mid-1800s, marks the descent's end at the Strafford village green.

Riding along Route 132 toward South Strafford, do not be surprised if you hear the sudden snorting of horses. Jumping competitions and other equestrian events are often held here, and you may arrive just in time for a show. Even if empty, these roadside pastures are worth a pause to behold.

The broad wooden steps in front of Coburn's General Store in South Strafford provide an opportunity to rest up for the ride's final 9 miles, along the Ompompanoosuc's western branch and across a covered bridge, back to Thetford Hill.

The Basics

Start: Thetford Hill. Take exit 14 off I-91 and follow Rte. 113 west for 1 mile. Park in the lot of the public school on the left.
Length: 51.4 miles.
Terrain: Hilly, with two climbs of almost 4 miles each.

Food: Two general stores in Chelsea, at 20.3 miles. Coburn's General Store in South Strafford at 42.7 miles.

Miles & Directions

- 0.0 From Thetford Hill proceed west on Rte. 113 toward Thetford Center.
- 5.0 Staying on Rte. 113, pass through Post Mills, following sign toward West Fairlee and Chelsea.
- 7.0 Pass through West Fairlee. Climb begins gradually.
- 12.5 Pass through Vershire. Climb steepens.
- 15.8 Climb ends at Ward's BP station. Begin descent to Chelsea.
- 20.3 Arriving in Chelsea, turn left on Rte. 110S toward Tunbridge. Hill's General Store and the Chelsea Country Store, established in 1818, are located side by side across from the town green on the right.
- 28.1 Cross bridge into Tunbridge and take an immediate sharp left turn. This unnamed road will quickly begin a nearly 4-mile climb.
- 31.9 Climb ends. Begin descent to South Strafford. Ride with caution; a portion of the road ahead is unpaved.
- 40.1 Left at Justin Morrill Smith monument, following the sign toward Chelsea, Tunbridge, and West Fairlee.
- 42.7 Left on Rte. 132 toward Union Village on arriving in South Strafford. The turn comes just after Coburn's General Store on the left.
- 47.0 Left on Tucker Hill Rd. just before Rte. 132 crosses a bridge over the west branch of the Ompompanoosuc River.
- 49.5 Cross covered bridge over Ompompanoosuc River.
- 50.0 Right on Rte. 113 at T.
- 51.4 Arrive at car, following a short climb back to Thetford Hill.

110

CHELSEA

113 Judgement Ridge

VERSHIRE

110

113

WEST
FAIRLEE

POST
MILLS

TUNBRIDGE

STRAFFORD

N

THETFORD
CENTER

SOUTH
STRAFFORD

132

RICES
MILLS

Tucker Hill

Road

113

THETFORD
HILL

Start / finish at
Public School

132

91

Connecticut River

43

Smuggler's Notch Challenge

- *Stowe—Mount Mansfield Forest*
  Smuggler's Notch—Jeffersonville
  Johnson—Hyde Park—Stowe

If the Kancamagus Highway across the White Mountains is New Hampshire's most scenic road, then Route 108 through Smuggler's Notch is the Green Mountain State's equivalent. From a cyclist's perspective especially, this claim is undeniably true. Steve Bushey of the Vermont Bicycle Touring company calls this loop through Smuggler's Notch one of New England's best. Steve is right. The Smuggler's Notch Challenge is a spectacular, exhilarating ride. Suitable for the intermediate or advanced cyclist only, it offers an experience that will not be forgotten.

Start with a warm-up stretch along the Stowe Recreation Path. Even those who normally disdain bike trails will like this one. Broad and smooth, it crisscrosses the West Branch of the Waterbury River. These opening 2 miles afford clear views of the mountains you will soon be riding through. The Pinnacle, Spruce Peak, Madonna Peak, and White Face mountains march northward. Towering behind them, 4,393-foot Mount Mansfield dominates the skyline. It is difficult to fathom from here just how a road can make its way through them.

Once you are on Route 108, the passage through Smuggler's Notch begins to reveal itself. The climb begins in earnest at 5 miles. The road enters a dense and cool woodland as it passes

---

244

the Mount Mansfield Ski Area. Farther along, it becomes clear why the Notch road is often closed in the winter months. Two steep switchbacks snake the road through a landscape of fern-covered glacial rubble.

Several bicycle races have in the past promoted the Notch road as their central challenge. Most riders, though, do not compete to get to the top. They shift into their easiest gear and take their time, enjoying the scenery on the way.

The rewards of this challenging 2-mile climb more than make up for the efforts expended on the way up. Cyclists can rest at the summit parking area, explore the hillside caves, or just take in the carnival atmosphere that prevails on warm afternoons. The Appalachian Trail crosses here, and the Notch is a popular staging point for hiking and camping expeditions.

Smuggler's Notch acquired its name during the War of 1812. Because it was remote enough not to be watched by revenue officers and had large caves for storage, the Notch became a favorite route for smugglers bringing contraband goods from Canada to Boston.

With its toughest climb behind, the Smuggler's Notch Challenge descends for 8 breathtaking miles to the Lamoille River and its three off-the-beaten-track valley towns. Jeffersonville, at the base of the descent, centers on a broad Main Street that is a pleasure to cycle slowly by. From there the Challenge follows back roads paralleling the Lamoille River (fine for fishing and canoeing). Route 15 then roller-coasters its way to Johnson, an old farming and industrial center where a woolen mill and talc plant were once the largest industries. Hyde Park, the last town on the way back to Stowe, was one of the earliest settlements in this region. Vermont's pioneers first cleared the forest here in 1787.

Stagecoach Road offers a final view toward Mount Mansfield and its neighbors. If you have already expended the energy you'd need to climb this last hill, the directions below give you the option of following Route 100, more heavily trafficked but flat, back to Stowe.

The Basics

Start: Stowe. Take exit 10 off I-89N. Drive 10 miles north on Rte. 100 through Waterbury Center. Park by the entrance to the Stowe Recreation Path, behind the white Community Church, on the left in the town center.
Length: 40.6 miles.
Terrain: One monster climb through Smuggler's Notch. Otherwise, rolling hills.
Food: The best choices are in Stowe, at the beginning or the end of the ride. There is a general store in Jeffersonville, at 14.5 miles. You may also want to pack a snack to eat on the banks of the Lamoille River, between 20 and 24 miles.

Miles & Directions

- 0.0 Start warming up along the Stowe Recreation Path, a wide paved path running parallel to but out of sight of Rte. 108N.
- 2.0 Recreation Path ends; join Rte. 108N.
- 4.8 Climb to Smuggler's Notch begins in earnest, with a steep half-mile step to the Mt. Mansfield Inn.
- 6.0 Enter Mt. Mansfield State Forest after a short downhill. Begin second step of climb, to the base of the Mt. Mansfield Ski Area.
- 6.3 Begin final stretch of climb. This last half mile features two narrow, exceedingly steep switchbacks.
- 6.8 Reach Smuggler's Notch, at 2,162 feet above sea level. Begin descent to Jeffersonville, almost 8 miles distant. The descent is steep but safe, without the tight switchbacks that marked the climb.
- 14.5 Enter Jeffersonville; bear right on Rte. 108 as it passes through the center of town.
- 15.0 On the far side of the Main St. stretch, bear left with Rte. 108, following the sign to Rte. 109. Cross Rte. 15 and the Lamoille River.

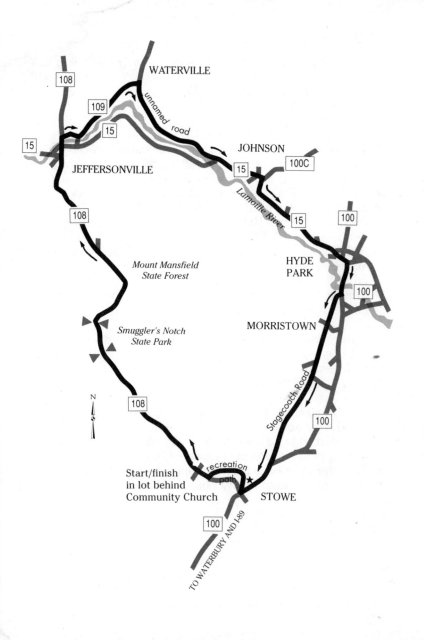

108

109

15

15

WATERVILLE

unnamed road

JOHNSON

100C

15

JEFFERSONVILLE

15

100

108

Lamoille River

15

Mount Mansfield
State Forest

HYDE
PARK

100

Smuggler's Notch
State Park

MORRISTOWN

N

108

Stagecoach Road

100

Start/finish
in lot behind
Community Church

recreation
path

STOWE

100

TO WATERBURY AND I-89

A scenic option here is to turn right on Rte. 15 and, in a half mile, take the first left, a cutoff to Rte. 109. This route will take you across the Lamoille River via one of Vermont's 108 covered bridges.

- 15.3 Right on Rte. 109 toward Waterville and Belvidere.
- 19.5 Right on an unnamed road 100 yards after crossing a small stream and just as Rte. 109 bears left toward Waterville. This is only the second possible right turn on Rte. 109.
- 24.0 Left on Rte. 15 toward Johnson and Hyde Park.
- 26.0 Pass through Johnson, staying on Rte. 15.
- 30.6 Turn right off Rte. 15 at sign for Hyde Park, then bear left into town.
- 31.1 Right, downhill, on unmarked street at the far end of Main St. Follow the sign toward Morristown. At bottom of hill, cross a dam over the Lamoille River.
- 31.8 Right, uphill, onto Stagecoach Rd., the back road to Stowe. It is unmarked here.

If you simply can't face another hill—and Stagecoach Rd. will climb steeply for a short while—continue straight, riding by Lamoille Lake. Then turn right onto Rte. 100, the main road back to Stowe.

- 33.1 Go straight through crossroads, staying on Stagecoach Rd. The hill ahead is the last of the ride. On the other side the road descends for 2 miles. You can still bail out, though, by turning left and sweeping downhill to Rte. 100.
- 39.0 Bear right onto Rte. 100, opposite the Foxfire Inn.
- 40.6 Arrive at Community Church in Stowe town center.

44

Northeast Kingdom Challenge

East Burke—West Burke—Westmore
East Charleston—East Haven—East Burke

From the summit of Burke Mountain, off Interstate 91 north of St. Johnsbury, a glaciated landscape of mountains, forests, lakes, and wide river valleys stretches toward the New Hampshire and Canadian borders. This is Vermont's Northeast Kingdom, as Senator George Aiken collectively dubbed the three still undeveloped and pristine counties of Orleans, Caledonia, and Essex back in 1948. By car or bike, follow the road up Burke Mountain, reached from Route 114 in East Burke, so that you may survey the domain before you set off on the Northeast Kingdom Challenge. Look especially for Lake Willoughby, visible through a mountain gap. It is a highlight of the tour.

The ride itself turns north on Route 5A after a 4-mile-long warm-up along a back road—and here one of the most famous scenes in Vermont unfolds. Ahead, mounts Hor and Pisgah rise abruptly from the otherwise gentle hills as a pair of solitary monadnocks. They are, respectively, the left and right rims of a U-shaped fold in the earth's crust.

Nestled between them, filling the trough, is 6-mile-long Lake Willoughby, universally regarded as one of the New England's most beautiful lakes. Its shores, for the most part surrounded by state park, are almost wholly undeveloped. The lake is stocked with fish, and the largest ever caught in Vermont, a thirty-four-pound brown trout, was taken from its 600-foot-deep waters. Twelve miles into the ride, as the road passes directly along the lake's bank beneath the cliffs of Mount Pisgah, a spring bubbles from the rocks on the right. Stop here to fill any empty water bottles. There is also a great lakeside swimming hole. Two general stores and short stretches of beautiful beach follow.

The ride started by following the course of the West Branch of the Passumpsic River toward Lake Willoughby. It ends with an equally long flat stretch following the course of the Passumpsic's East Branch back to East Burke. The miles in between roll across several long but gradual climbs. Carry all the food you may need, as the ride's second half passes through remote countryside.

Vermont Country Cyclers leads a five-day inn-to-inn cycling odyssey through the Northeast Kingdom. The Northeast Kingdom Challenge is a modified version of the route guests follow on one of those days. Their actual route begins in Montgomery Center, crosses Jay Peak, and continues one-way past Lake Willoughby to East Burke. A van carries everyone's baggage and stops to serve a prepared lunch midway.

Accommodations in East Burke include the Wildflower Inn, a refurbished farmhouse just south of town, and the Old Cutter Inn, located on the road leading to the Burke Mountain Ski Area on the north side of town. For those who prefer to camp, nearby Darling State Park, open from Memorial Day to mid-October, boasts thirty tent sites, facilities (hot showers!), and a camp store. As with any ride starting far from home, be certain to reserve accommodations in advance. The St. Johnsbury Chamber of Commerce can provide you with additional lodging referrals.

The Basics

Start: East Burke. Driving north, take exit 23 off I-91 into Lyndonville. Follow Rte. 5 north through Lyndonville, then turn right onto Rte. 114 for the final 4 miles to East Burke. Arriving from the north, take exit 24 onto Rte. 122S into Lyndonville. Then turn north onto routes 5 and 114 to East Burke. Ride distances are measured from Bailey's General Store in the center of town.

Length: 55.5 or 65.5 miles.

Terrain: Gently rolling backcountry roads with several long flat stretches.

Food: Two general stores and plentiful picnic spots along the shores of Lake Willoughby, starting at 11.0 miles. The East Charleston Store at 30.0 miles is the only possible snack stop on the ride's long second half.

Miles & Directions

- 0.0 From Bailey's General Store in the center of East Burke, ride south on Rte. 114 just a short distance and then turn right onto the side road toward Burke Hollow and West Burke. This turnoff is directly opposite the Old School Museum, a former schoolhouse that now houses interesting relics of Vermont's past. Immediately cross bridge and turn right toward Burke Hollow. The ride starts with a short climb and descent.
- 2.9 Descending with caution into Burke Hollow, bear left and then immediately turn right to stay on the main road.
- 4.1 Bear left across a small river as you enter West Burke.
- 4.2 Right onto Rte. 5A-N at stop sign. Stay on Rte. 5A for the next 19.4 miles, including 6 miles along the shore of Lake Willoughby. No major climbs until after passing the lake.
- 11.0 Lake Willoughby. This 6-mile-long lake, wedged between the sheer faces of Mt. Pisgah on the right and Mt. Hor on the left, was dug out by glaciers ages ago.
- 12.2 Spring on the right and great swimming from the rocks on the left. Fill water bottles here, if needed.
- 17.8 Stay right with Rte. 5A as Rte. 58 turns left toward Orleans. Continuing north from Lake Willoughby, this circuit passes through some of the Northeast Kingdom's most undeveloped areas.

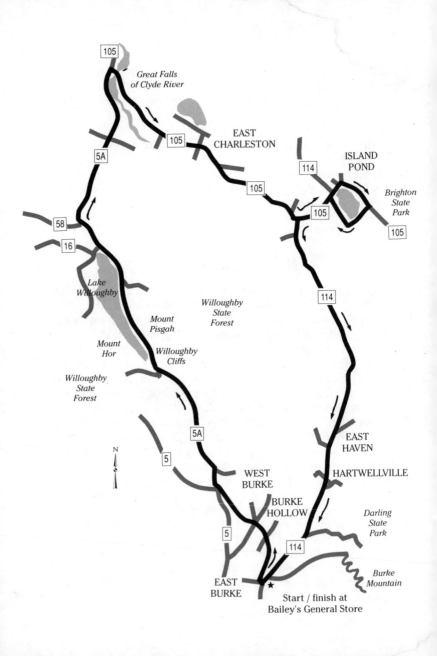

105

*Great Falls
of Clyde River*

105

EAST
CHARLESTON

114

ISLAND
POND

105

*Brighton
State
Park*

5A

105

58

105

16

114

*Lake
Willoughby*

*Willoughby State
Forest*

*Mount
Pisgah*

*Mount
Hor*

*Willoughby
Cliffs*

*Willoughby
State
Forest*

N

5A

5

EAST
HAVEN

HARTWELLVILLE

*Darling
State
Park*

WEST
BURKE

BURKE
HOLLOW

5

114

EAST
BURKE

*Burke
Mountain*

★

Start / finish at
Bailey's General Store

- 24.0 Right at junction onto Rte. 105S toward East Charleston and Island Pond. Immediately cross the Clyde River, whose Great Falls cascade through a gorge to the left. Stay on Rte. 105 for the next 10.1 gradually rolling miles.
- 30.0 East Charleston Store on the right. Last stop for food and water.
- 35.0 Right onto Rte. 114S toward Burke Mountain.

To add roughly 10 miles and a scenic detour to this ride, bear left onto combined routes 114N and 105E to Island Pond and Brighton State Park. Turn right onto Rte. 105E in the town of Island Pond. Then turn right off Rte. 105 to Brighton State Park. Continuing around Island Pond after visiting the park itself, turn left onto combined routes 114S and 105W. Then turn left to continue on Rte. 114S back to East Burke.

- 44.0 Pass through small village of East Haven.
- 55.2 Pass turnoff for Burke Mountain Ski Area to the left.
- 55.5 Return to Bailey's General Store in East Burke.

Appendix

Bicycle Touring and Racing Clubs in New England

In cycling's second century, its popularity as a group recreation and sport is at a new peak. New England is home to dozens of cycling teams, clubs, and outing groups, ranging from the small bike shop club to organizations with several hundred members.

In addition to organizing regular, normally weekly, rides for members, nearly every established cycling club promotes a premier ride intended to attract cyclists from throughout a region. Some of these tours have become so popular that they have won a nationwide following. The annual *Bicycle USA Almanac,* published by the League of American Wheelmen, lists hundreds of such tours nationwide. They range from the Arctic Bicycle Club's Chena Hot Springs Classic to the Florida Freewheelers' Horrible Hundred ride. Attracting dozens and even hundreds of cyclists, they are commonly mapped as century (100-mile), metric century (62-mile), or half century (50-mile) rides. September is the traditional century ride season.

New England's many clubs host their share of spectacular cycling expeditions. Rhode Island's Narragansett Bay Wheelmen club is famous for its annual Flattest Century in the East. Boston's Charles River Wheelmen offer a half-dozen different routes during their annual Spring Century weekend. Maine's Penobscot Wheelmen invite riders north for the Poulin Century. New Hampshire's Granite State Wheelmen host the Tri-State Seacoast Century, which challenges the Rhode Island club's claim to the flattest ride. And Vermont provides a welcome to the eighty hardy cyclists who take on the annual Tour of Scenic

Rural Vermont, a two-day double century included in this collection of the best bike rides in New England.

If you would like to find out more about organized club rides anywhere in the country, write or call the League of American Wheelmen, the umbrella organization for clubs like those mentioned here. The following listing provides the names and addresses of New England's most established racing and touring groups. Contact your local bicycle shop, the United States Cycling Federation (for racing), or the League of American Wheelmen (for touring) for more information.

National Cycling Organizations

The League of American Wheelmen
Suite 209
6707 Whitestone Rd.
Baltimore, MD 21207
(301) 944–3399

United States Cycling Federation
1750 East Boulder St.
Colorado Springs, CO 80909
(719) 578–4581

Connecticut Cycling Organizations

Touring

Coalition of Connecticut Bicyclists
205 Foster St.
New Haven, CT 06511

Middlesex Bicycle Club
126 Highland Ave.
Middletown, CT 06457

Pequot Cyclists
P.O. Box 505
Gales Ferry, CT 06335

Sound Cyclists Bicycle Club
2625 Park Ave., #15A
Bridgeport, CT 06604

Racing

BRNO Velo
P.O. Box 4378
Greenwich, CT 06830

Capitol Velo Club
57 Welles St.
Glastonbury, CT 06033

Central Connecticut Cycling Club
39 Manitook Dr.
Oxford, CT 06483

Exposition Wheelmen
178 West Middle Turnpike
Manchester, CT 06040

Full Cycle Road Club
1030 Main St.
Newington, CT 06111

Laurel Bicycle Club
421 East Main St.
Meriden, CT 06450

Les Cyclistes
68 Bayberry Hill Rd.
Ridgefield, CT 06877

Pequot Cyclists
57 Three Bridges Rd.
East Haddam, CT 06423

Maine Cycling Organizations

Touring

Casco Bay Bicycle Club
82 Wellington Rd.
Portland, ME 04103

Penobscot Wheelmen
260 Main St.
Waterville, ME 04901

Commercial Touring Companies

Maine Coast Cyclers
P.O. Box 1234

Camden, ME 04843
(802) 496–4603

Massachusetts Cycling Organizations

Touring

American Youth Hostels
1020 Commonwealth Ave.
Boston, MA 02215
(617) 731–5430

Appalachian Mountain Club
5 Joy St.
Boston, MA 02108
(617) 523–0636
(Some local chapters lead
bicycle tours.)

Boston Area Bicycle Coalition
P.O. Box 1015
Cambridge, MA 02142

Charles River Wheelmen
19 Chase Ave.
West Newton, MA 02165

Cyclonauts Bicycling Club
29 Brooklawn Rd.
Wilbraham, MA 01095

Fitchburg Cycling Club, Inc.
P. O. Box 411
Lunenburg, MA 01462

Franklin-Hampshire
Freewheelers
RFD 3, Two Mile Rd.
Amherst, MA 01002

Nashoba Valley Pedalers
P.O. Box 398
Acton, MA 01720

Seven Hills Wheelmen
Box 24, Greendale Station
Worcester, MA 01606

Racing

Boston Road Club
58 Berwick St.
Belmont, MA 02178

CCB International
102 Broadway
Saugus, MA 01906

Cyclonauts Racers
P. O. Box 743
Wilbraham, MA 01095

East Bay Cycling Club
20 Angell St.
Attleboro, MA 02703

Elan Velo Club
Life Sports-East India Mall
Salem, MA 01970

Mass Bay Road Club
P. O. Box 791
Plymouth, MA 02360

Missing Link Bicycle Club
230 Washington St.
Weymouth, MA 02188

Northeast Bicycle Club, Inc.
1580 Massachusetts Ave.
Lexington, MA 02173

Pioneer Valley Racing Group
52 Riverview Ave.
Longmeadow, MA 01106

Worcester Road Club
230 Chestnut Hill Rd.
Holden, MA 01520

New Hampshire Cycling Organizations

Touring

Granite State Wheelmen
16 Clinton St.
Salem, NH 03079

North Shore Cyclists
41 Maple Ave.
Newton, NH 03858

Peaked Mountain Bicycle
Club
P.O. Box 102
Piermont, NH 03779

Racing ·

Nashua Velo Club
P.O. Box 3566
Nashua, NH 03061

Sunapee/Mowatt Bike Club
162 North Main
Newport, NH 03773

*Commercial Touring
Companies*

New Hampshire Bicycle
Touring
10 Maple St.
P.O. Box 547
Henniker, NH 03242
(603) 428–7500

Rhode Island Cycling Organizations

Touring

Narragansett Bay Wheelmen
P.O. Box 1317
Providence, RI 02901

Vermont Cycling Organizations

Touring

Three Banana Bicycle Club
4 Spring St.
St. Johnsbury, VT 05819

Racing

Green Mountain Bicycle Club
12 Maple St.
Essex Junction, VT 05452

Stowe Bicycle Club
RR 2, Box 280
Stowe, VT 05672

*Commercial Touring
Companies*

Vermont Bicycle Touring
Box 711-AV
Bristol, VT 05443
(802) 453–4811

Vermont Country Cyclers
Dept. 330038, Box 145
Waterbury Center, VT 05677
(802) 244–5215